VISUAL PROCESSING

COMPUTATIONAL, PSYCHOPHYSICAL, AND COGNITIVE RESEARCH

Visual Processing:
Computational, Psychophysical, and Cognitive Research

R. J. Watt

MRC Applied Psychology Unit, 15 Chaucer Road, Cambridge, U.K.

LAWRENCE ERLBAUM ASSOCIATES, PUBLISHERS
Hove and London (UK)   Hillsdale (USA)

Lawrence Erlbaum Associates Ltd., Publishers
27 Palmeira Mansions
Church Road
Hove
East Sussex, BN3 2FA
U.K.

Pub: Hove, U.K.: Erlbaum, 1988

British Library Cataloguing in Publication Data

Watt, R.J.
  Visual processing : computational,
  psychophysical and cognitive research. / R. J. Watt
  1. Visual perception
  I. Title   xiii, ill., 152 p.
  152.1'4   References: 146-148

ISBN 0-86377-081-9

Typeset by Latimer Trend & Company Ltd, Plymouth
Printed and bound by A. Wheaton & Co. Ltd., Exeter

For Helen

Contents

Acknowledgements

Many people have contributed to this essay. Some did so unwittingly by making opportune comments out of context: Issues of representation are similar whether it is visual space or creative thoughts or emotions that are to be described by the representation. Others have more deliberately challenged the crude ideas that eventually led to the arguments of this essay, and I would especially like to record my gratitude to D. Andrews, D. Foster, S. Laughlin, and M. Morgan.

I should like to thank A. Baddeley, V. Bruce, B. Craven, P. Johnson-Laird, B. Moulden, D. Osorio, T. Valentine, and A. Wilkins for their critical comments on the presentation of my ideas. Valda Jones typed, retyped, reretyped this until she was blue in the face. I shall be eternally grateful.

Preface: Scope and Purpose of this Essay

Vision seems effortless and simple to us, the users. We can sense the shape, structure, and spatial layout of a large number of remote objects very rapidly and usually with a high level of accuracy and stability. Our only conscious actions are to point the eyes in the right direction, focus them, and apply the ephemeral commodity of attention to items of especial interest or importance. Even these actions seem effortless in normal use: when scanning a road before stepping off the pavement; or when reading text, examining graphs, watching the television.

It has, however, been found to be extremely difficult to make machinery that can form images from light already available in the environment, and then interpret such images in terms of the three-dimensional scene. The failure to build a general-purpose vision system has many roots, some of which are particularly instructive with important lessons on how not to think about vision. For instance, it is quite usual to start with two cameras and then to recover range (depth) data from the geometry of stereopsis. After all, we have two eyes in our head, and obviously need both for the vivid stereoscopic sensation of depth. But is depth perception the real reason why we have two eyes? Perhaps we have two eyes to allow for mechanical faults, and indeed more than 10% of the population of Western countries (and much higher proportions in Third World countries) have a fault in one eye that renders it useless. This is the condition known as amblyopia, and the perception of distance by amblyopes is not impaired to any significant extent. The lesson for engineers is that they should avoid unnecessary preconceptions and perhaps consider using three or even more cameras; the lesson for psychologists is that introspection is a very blunt scientific instrument.

It is not surprising, given the ease with which we see and the immense difficulty in emulating it, that rather little is known of our visual system and its actions. The root obstacle to progress has been the lack of a sufficiently general definition of what vision does. On the one hand it has been studied indirectly as the sense that is used when reading language. It has also been studied as the sense that can accomplish two-dimensional pattern recognition and judge whether patterns of markings are similar or different. It has been involved in studies of motor behaviour, concerned with the co-ordination and control of actions by visual information. In many psychophysical studies, it is used because it is there—the underlying philosophy being that the visual system exists to discriminate small differences between patterns of luminance.

A notable exception to these generalisations was the late David Marr, whose 1982 book has marked a new chapter in research. The central point that Marr has communicated so effectively is that vision is actually impossible unless one knows a great deal about how the environment is, or should be, constrained. Atoms tend to clump into relatively large, stable, smoothly surfaced bodies, for example. The general philosophy that I adopt in this essay is the same but with two differences. The first is a concern for detailed findings of quantitative psychophysical experiments as well as results from more cognitive approaches to vision. The second, which is important from the third chapter of this essay onwards, is a consideration of what is meant by the notions of visual measurements (e.g. of edge blur and position). These two differences lead to a very different appreciation of the initial stages of human vision from that proposed by Marr (e.g. 1976).

In the first chapter of this essay I start by defining the scope of the early levels of vision that are called Primal Sketch visual processing. Imagine a real optical image of the scene around you: This has variations in light intensity that arise because of the shape, colour, and texture of the surfaces in the scene, and the layout of the bodies in the scene, as well as the layout of the light sources. The Primal Sketch is concerned to recover and register as many of these variations in intensity as it can. Such a record of the image provides a rich source of information concerning the layout of bodies in the scene and their nature. The task of the Primal Sketch, therefore, is also to organise the information into a representation that is meaningful for further analysis and action. The first chapter of this essay examines the computational theory of how this may be done.

The second and third chapters of this essay explore the implications of the computational analysis for the interpretation of psychophysical data and models. Since this essay is principally an exposition of my own point of view, Chapter 2 is based on the MIRAGE model of Watt and Morgan (1985).

Chapter 3 addresses the question of just what it means to say that the visual system measures spatial aspects of the retinal image, such as the length and orientation of lines. The central concern in this chapter is the effects of distortions introduced by the processes of finding edges and lines, and how these distortions can be corrected or avoided. This is generally possible for image attributes that fall into reliable and characteristic distributions, for which error-correcting codes are applicable. Spatial position is an attribute for which this technique is not applicable. In Marr's scheme the position or visual direction of an edge is simply determined by the location of a zero-crossing in an image plane. This assumes good image geometry, an assumption that I question.

The fourth and fifth chapters then consider the issues of grouping and dynamic control, and I believe these to be the reward for the reader who has persevered so far. The line of argument up to this point stresses the computational requirements of the system and its psychophysical performance. The need for structured representation and dynamic control at a very early stage in the sequence of processes can be traced back logically to the nature of the physical environment. In the fifth chapter I observe a similarity between the behaviour of the Primal Sketch, in its new form, and the phenomena of visual attention.

The synthesis that results is recapitulated in the final chapter. I would claim that the strength of the link between the low-level approaches of psychophysics and computational theory and the high-level approaches of cognitive visual function lies in the logic of the arguments that indicate the computational need for control. It is a strong claim that the computational approach and the psychophysics have built a sufficiently constrained and powerful model of the early stages of vision to make it sensible and meaningful to enquire how much of the supposedly higher-level aspects of the psychology of vision can be accounted for thereby.

I think that it is now necessary to re-examine the usefulness of a distinction between high-level and low-level processes in vision. If high-level control of early processing stages is a feature of the system, to what extent can those early stages be regarded as low-level? The concept of high- and low-level aspects to a visual task is a rather different issue and is clearly a valid distinction. It does not follow that these will map onto distinct high- and low-level processing stages within the system.

1

Introduction

Light is the freely available messenger that allows us to sense remote objects in our environment without the need to interact with them directly. This is the modern view of vision that began with the Persian philosopher and physicist, Alhazen (or more properly, abu-'Ali Al Hasen ibn Al Haytham, 965–1039). Vision would have been easier to understand if the older view that light is emitted by the eye as a type of feeler, had been correct. Laser range finders work on this principle and are at present the only flawless way of measuring depth with light images. In the same way the colour of a surface, i.e. its reflectance, is easily computed if you know the position and nature of the source of light and the orientation of the surface.

The more difficult modern view, however, is the accepted version, and much of the rest of this essay will be concerned with the effects of unknown sources of light on an unknown arrangement of surfaces in the scene. Light is an uncertain messenger: It is not like a nice steady weight that can be reliably measured; it is a stream of random and largely independent particles, the photons, each of which has its own characteristic energy. The rate of arrival of photons at the eye is variable; we call this photon noise, and the variability depends on the mean rate. The mean rate of arrival is the intensity of the light. It is usually expressed as intensity per unit area, illuminance, which is similar to luminance, the intensity per unit area of emitted light. To avoid these cumbersome photometric units, I shall use the term grey-level to refer to the illuminance of the retina at an arbitrary small area.

In vision, measurements of the intensity of light sources are not of interest.

The source is incidental; the major interest is the disposition of reflecting surfaces in three-dimensional space. Light from the sources is reflected at surfaces, perhaps many times, and some eventually enters the eye. The grey-level or intensity at a particular place in the retinal image is determined by the output and positions of the sources, the reflectance, depth, and orientation of the surface imaged at that point with respect to the sources and the observer, and any mutual illumination of surfaces (i.e. light reflected from one surface to another, which is then illuminated directly from the source and also indirectly via the first surface).

If one knows all these details, then the grey-level at that particular point in the image can be calculated. The problem in vision is that these processes cannot be reversed: The grey-level on its own does not distinguish between the various factors causing it. In principle, any given retinal image could arise from an infinity of possible scenes, including a flat uniform surface illuminated by a patterned light source (the principle behind slide and cine projection). In practice, of course, we are very rarely faced with any operational ambiguity. The visual system generally manages to make a choice concerning the scene, and it is usually correct. This choice is made on the basis of assumptions concerning the most likely types of scenes. The scenes that we inhabit are generally constrained.

OUTPUT REQUIREMENTS OF VISUAL PROCESSING

Vision exists so that we can see what to do. Ultimately visual tasks require a full scene description in terms of the visible bodies, their shapes and sizes, their positions and motions, and their surface colours and markings. We are a long way from understanding how this is done, but we can, for simplicity's sake, break the process down into a number of sub-processes.

Marr's analysis of the architecture of low-level vision is currently the most widely used (see Marr, 1982), even though there are doubts about many details. Marr divided the process of vision down into three sub-processes, each of which delivers a representation for the next sub-processes. The three representations may be summarized as:

Primal Sketch:	A two-dimensional representation of significant grey-level changes in the image.
2.5D Sketch:	A partial three-dimensional representation recording surface distances from the observer.
Solid-model based representation:	A fully worked out volumetric representation of bodies in the scene.

There are significant concepts in this simple framework. A *representation* is a symbolic descriptor. It builds a description from a finite *alphabet of primitive symbols* (such as "edge", "bar", "corner"), each having an associated attribute list (recording: size, orientation, contrast, for example) and a *grammar* or set of rules that will exactly and exclusively generate all valid *sentences* or scene descriptions. A *sketch* is the process that produces, analyses, and represents the data.

This essay is concerned only with the Primal Sketch, the reason being that there are several psychophysical and psychological studies that indicate that the Primal Sketch is far from dull and straightforward. Whereas Marr tended to regard it as an inflexible, automatic, memoryless process producing something rather like an edge map, I shall describe some evidence that points to high-level control and memory very early in the process. It will be argued that many of the visual attention phenomena have their roots, trunk, and some branches in the Primal Sketch, and that there is a particularly striking simplicity to the machinery that belies a wonderfully rich diversity of function.

Output Requirements of the Primal Sketch

Why have a Primal Sketch? Why not just have a 2.5D Sketch as the first stage? The motive for the existence of a separate Primal Sketch in Marr's work is relatively simple. The image itself has a great deal of information that is irrelevant to the 2.5D Sketch, and the Primal Sketch can be used to provide an economical representation. A second reason is that many of the computational problems in the 2.5D Sketch, such as stereomatching, would be hopelessly confounded by grey-levels rather than, for example, edge tokens. To these two reasons, one can add the obvious statement that many visual processes require a representation of the grey-level changes, not a 2.5D Sketch. Imagine how text would have to be written if we had no access to a Primal Sketch.

It seems reasonable to require that the Primal Sketch squeeze as much meaningful information out of the image as possible. Only part of this will be relevant for the 2.5D Sketch. One ultimate goal of vision is an understanding of the layout of bodies in three-dimensional space. The term *body* is used here to refer to a compact solid mass that remains coherent, at least over the time scale of perception. Our perceptual understanding of the scene is going to be in terms of objects, which do not necessarily correspond to bodies. A tree in winter is one body, but may be represented as a hierarchy of objects: its overall bulk, the trunk, and largest boughs, or individual twigs. The term *object* refers to a unit of perception. Bodies cause the input to vision; objects cause behaviour that is the output of vision.

The main task of the Primal Sketch is therefore to extract from the image all the relevant information about the layout and character of visible surfaces and to construct a convenient representation. Ideally the representation at this level of processing will be used in turn for all other subsequent processes, and so it must be a rich source of information. The Primal Sketch representation will be used to construct a depth representation, using for example information about occlusions, shading, texture gradients, and disparity differences (if there are two Primal Sketches, one per eye). The interesting parts of images concern the locations where surfaces become occluded, especially where surfaces occlude themselves by turning away from the observer, and the locations where surfaces bend even though they may remain visible, such as sharp creases.

Figure 1.1 shows a ground plan for a scene and marks the position of an observer, O. The scene has three walls, W_1-W_4, within which there are five bodies: an upright circular cylinder, C; two boxes with rectangular cross-sections, S, R; an upright block with triangular cross-section, T; and a sphere, B. Various lines-of-sight from the observer are also shown and each reaches a point of particular interest, which we might require the Primal Sketch to identify. For example, the cylinder occludes itself at points C_1 and C_2. There is no sudden change in the character of the cylinder surface here, but to the observer, these two points will appear to be distinctive as the edges of the cylinder because there is a discontinuity in surface depth from the observer. Very often such occluding edges also correspond to discontinuities in surface orientation, i.e. *creases* or *corners*, such as points R_1, R_3, and W_1. Creases and corners can also be imaged so that they do not correspond to the occluding edges of objects, as at points T_2 and R_2.

The top of Fig. 1.2 shows the equivalent range or depth map for the observer at point O. This might be a useful precursor to a full reconstruction of Fig. 1.1 because it records the distance from O to the nearest reflecting surface in each direction. Figure 1.2 also shows the variation in the orientation of the visible surfaces in the scene with respect to the observer at O. Surface orientation is important because it determines the surface luminance: Surfaces that are head-on to the source of light have a higher illumination level per unit surface area than those oblique to the source. Notice that the lines-of-sight from the observer to occluding edges correspond to sudden changes in range from the observer and sometimes also in orientation. The lines-of-sight to creases, such as T_2 and R_2, correspond to abrupt changes in surface orientation, but not in range.

We could start by requiring that the Primal Sketch discover as many points in the image that correspond to these interesting lines-of-sight as possible. We can go further and, expecting that many surfaces will have textured markings on them, ask that some measure of the variations in texture grain size over each surface patch be made, so that the shape and orientation of the surface and its edges can be subsequently assessed. These requirements can be summarised by stating that the Primal Sketch should produce a representation of the image in which features corresponding to surface creases and discontinuities are recorded, along with their shape,

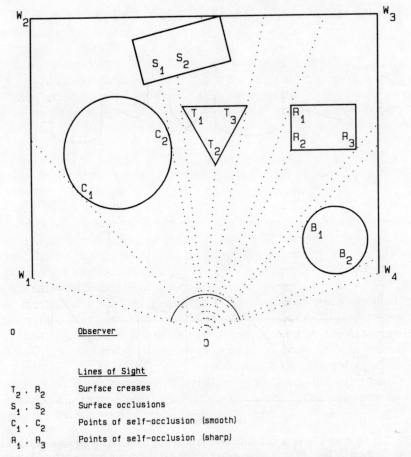

FIG. 1.1.   A plan of an imaginary scene. The image formed by the observer at O will contain segments corresponding in sequence to the various visible surfaces. These segments are bounded by the lines-of-sight that are drawn from O to each point of surface occlusion or surface creasing. The problem for the Primal Sketch is to discover these lines-of-sight from the image and then to represent their spatial relations and their nature or probable cause (i.e. occlusion or crease).

orientation, and relative locations. The representation should also record variations in surface texture.

CONSTRAINTS ON THE INPUT TO THE PRIMAL SKETCH

The task just defined for the Primal Sketch would be hopelessly difficult except for the fact that natural surfaces are generally homogeneous in colour

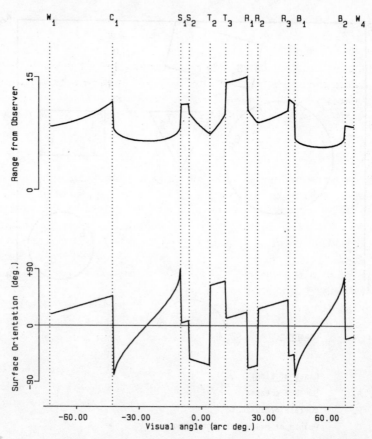

FIG. 1.2. A range map (top) and surface orientation map (bottom) for the scene of Fig. 1.1 from the point *O*. The different surface segments shown in that figure now correspond to areas where range and surface orientation change smoothly, and the segment boundaries are marked by sharp changes of direction and discontinuities in these maps.

and texture, and that these properties vary from surface to surface. As a result, any place in the image where the *nature of the reflected light changes suddenly* is likely to correspond to an occluding edge, although there are several caveats.

It is only usually the case that changes in reflected light indicate surface discontinuities or creases: Shadows very often cause a larger change in luminance than surface discontinuities, for example. However, the nature of the reflected light may not change very much at a shadow in terms of its spectral content or texture, which are predominantly determined by the surface itself. If the change in reflected light is sudden, then it is unlikely to be a shadow or a slowly varying gradient of illumination. But recall that all light is carried by random photons. Adding photon noise to an image is the same as adding a random number to the grey-level value of every point in the image. There will always be sudden changes between adjacent points, so it is not sufficient to detect sudden changes in grey-level in the image. A phrase like "sudden and consistent on average" has to be employed instead to imply that surfaces generally occupy large areas of the image, whereas noise fluctuations are very restricted in size.

Luminance and Surfaces

Return to the scene of Fig. 1.1. How does the luminance of the various surfaces in the scene vary? Luminance depends on both the surface reflectance (colour), which is a property of the surface, and how it is illuminated. Let us suppose that they all have the same Lambertian reflectance, which is the most difficult condition for a visual system to deal with. All the surfaces are the same shade of matt grey. Let us also start with the case where there is a single point source of light at the position O. In this case there are no shadows visible to the observer.

Figure 1.3 shows the variations in grey-level along a one-dimensional slice through the image formed of the scene by the observer at O. These variations in grey-level are equivalent to variations in surface luminance, and in keeping with common practice, I shall use the terms luminance and grey-level synonymously when referring to an image. The variations in luminance arise because the distance of the surfaces from the source varies and because luminance is reduced by an amount depending on the angle of incidence of the light on the surface.

Inspection of Fig. 1.3 suggests that where surface creases and discontinuities exist, a sharp corner in the luminance profile can be expected. At such sharp corners, luminance slope changes suddenly (discontinuously). The first derivative of a function specifies its rate of change or slope at each point. It is found by taking each luminance value and subtracting the luminance value to be found a very small distance to its left (leftwards is only a convention; rightwards would produce the same result, multiplied by -1 and shifted very slightly). Discontinuities in the first derivative are places where there is a sudden large change in its value, and these can be easily detected by looking for isolated large deviations from zero (positive and negative) in the derivative of the first derivative, that is, in the second derivative of the luminance profile. The second panel of Fig. 1.3 shows the second derivative: For each of the marked scene features, there is an isolated peak and/or trough in this function.

To summarise, changes in luminance are important because they are related to surface orientation and reflectance. Where the rate of change itself changes suddenly, the visual system can learn about changes in surface

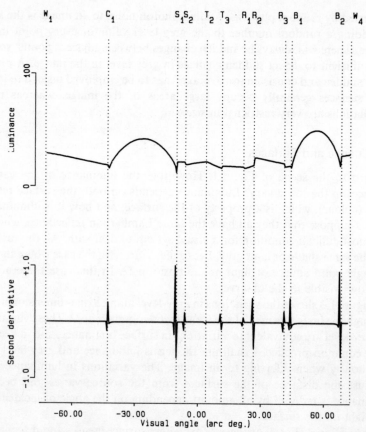

FIG. 1.3. The top of this figure shows the luminance profile of the image formed of the scene at the point O. The different surface segments shown in the figure now correspond to areas where luminance changes smoothly. The bottom of the figure shows the second derivative of the luminance profile. Surface creases and discontinuities are now marked by sharp peaks in this new signal.

orientation. Changes in a rate of change are measured by taking second derivatives.

This has been a consideration of a special case where the only source of light is illumination from a *point source*. How about more general conditions of illumination? For most scenes, there are a small number of relatively remote sources of light. Initially these sources provide *parallel illumination* as the light strikes the scene surfaces, so the surface luminances due to this depend on the direction of the light source. Light reflected off all the surfaces is scattered through the scene and provides secondary illumination of each surface. This is much less directional and effectively becomes *diffuse illumination*, which can be regarded as normal (i.e. perpendicular) to any and all surfaces. The surface luminances due to this do not depend on where the light sources are, but depend only on surface reflectance. There are therefore two other special cases to consider: diffuse illumination and parallel illumination. In the case of diffuse illumination, all surfaces will be under the same illuminance, and the luminance in the image due to this will just be a function of surface reflectances.

The other special case concerns illumination from a remote source so that the direction of illumination is parallel over the scene. This is illustrated in Fig. 1.4, and, as can be seen, shadows will be formed behind each body in the

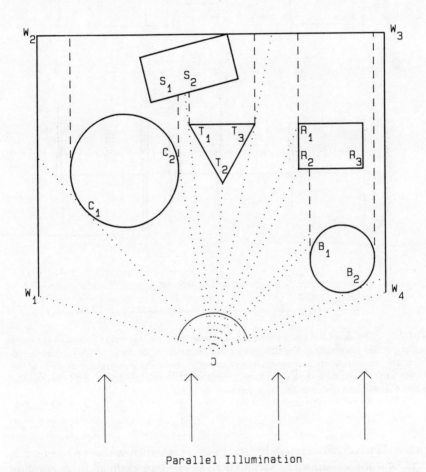

Parallel Illumination

FIG. 1.4.   A plan of the imaginary scene of Fig. 1.1 showing the effects of parallel illumination of the scene from a remote source of light. Shadows are cast behind each of the bodies as shown by the parallel dashed lines, and some of these will be visible to the observer at O as dark regions on the surfaces. Secondary illumination by light reflected at the various surfaces will be cast on those areas not directly illuminated by the source, but it will be much weaker and not directional.

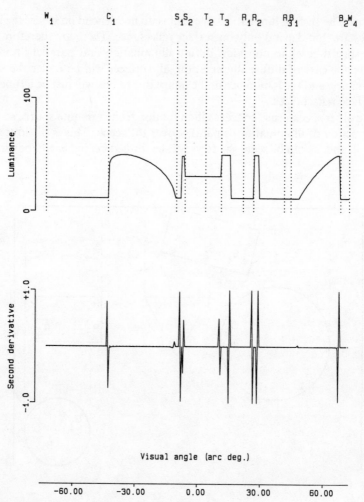

FIG. 1.5.   The top of this figure shows the luminance profile of the image formed of the scene under parallel illumination. The different surface segments in the scene no longer correspond invariably to areas where luminance changes smoothly, since shadows are cast on some of the visible surfaces and these show up as large luminance discontinuities that do not correspond to surface creases and discontinuities (e.g. between T_3 and R_1).

scene. The luminance image for such a scene is shown in the top of Fig. 1.5, and beneath it is drawn its second derivative. Once again all the interesting features except those in the shade (e.g. R_3) cause peaks and troughs in the second derivative. This time however, the edges of shadows, such as that between T_3 and R_1, also cause peaks.

In general, illumination in any scene is a mixture of the three special cases we have considered, and it is possible to say that each surface discontinuity or crease will usually cause a peak and/or trough in the second derivative of the image luminance waveform. Inspecting Figs. 1.3 and 1.5, it is possible to distinguish three different luminance configurations. There are *luminance discontinuities* (as at R_1, R_2); there are *luminance gradient discontinuities* (as at T_2 in Fig. 1.3); and there are *luminance peaks* and troughs (as at C_1, S_1 in Fig. 1.3). Luminance peaks are really a combination of a luminance discontinuity and a luminance gradient discontinuity. It should be noted that each luminance discontinuity causes *a peak and a trough*, whereas a luminance gradient discontinuity causes either *a peak or trough* in the second derivative. Moreover, the peak and trough arising from a luminance discontinuity are actually on either side of it, not aligned with it. This makes it possible to identify whether a luminance discontinuity or luminance gradient discontinuity in the original image is responsible for any particular second derivative sharp peak. Figure 1.6 shows what the second derivatives of a variety of different luminance profiles look like. The top three are types of luminance gradient discontinuities, where luminance is not discontinuous and in each case an isolated sharp peak is found in the second derivative. I shall refer to these as luminance *lines* in the image. The lower three are luminance discontinuities, and in each case the second derivative is an isolated pair of opposite polarity sharp peaks only infinitesimally separated. I shall refer to these as luminance *edges* in the image. It is these two different arrangements that allow the second derivative to be interpreted.

The argument so far can be summarised by saying that we have noted a constraint on the appearance of luminance values in images, such that the second derivative of luminance shows sharp peaks and troughs at points of interest in the image (i.e. surface creases and discontinuities). Shadows will, of course, behave like surface discontinuities if they are sharp enough; and illumination highlights will tend to produce peaks in the second derivative, although these will only be sharp if the surface is specularly reflecting (has a glossy or metallic finish so that the light source is actually reflected directionally by the surface rather than scattered diffusely).

It should be pointed out that this argument runs rather differently from that of Marr and Hildreth (1980) or most standard approaches to edge-finding in images (e.g. Canny, 1984), where the starting point is to define an abrupt step change in luminance as the standard edge and to design detectors to find all the occurrences of such a feature in images. Our consideration of a simple image has led to a different luminance feature because we are seeking creases as well as occlusions. As a consequence, it is most convenient to detect peaks/troughs in the second derivative, whereas Canny and others prefer peaks in the first derivative. Marr and Hildreth used a second derivative operator, but detected zero-crossings in its output: This is formally the same

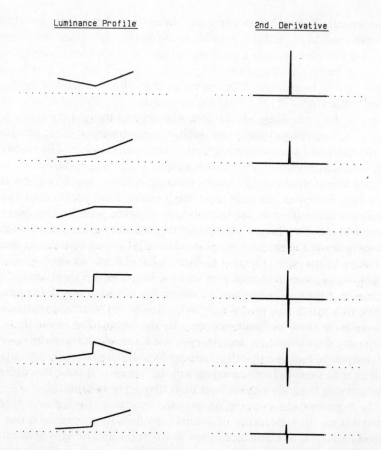

Luminance Profile   2nd. Derivative

FIG. 1.6.   Assorted luminance waveforms, all with discontinuities in gradient or in luminance. On the right are shown the corresponding second derivatives. Note that each luminance discontinuity gives rise to two peaks of opposite signs in the second derivative, whereas luminance gradient discontinuities give rise to only one peak. This difference would allow an interpretation of the image structure.

as detecting a peak in a first derivative. One exception to this trend is found in the work of Pearson and Robinson (1985). They were interested in the practical problem of producing a binary (black and white only) image of a person's face and hands so that deaf-and-dumb people could use standard telephone lines for communication. Pearson and Robinson wanted to send a moving cartoon of the sign language, and they found a solution similar to the one previously outlined. They used troughs in the second derivative of a front-lit image of the face and hands, viewed against a light background, so that all those parts that were slanting away from the light and camera would be detected because they are darker than their surrounds. This method is not sensitive to all of the interesting parts of images, but is very suitable for their problem.

Texture and Surfaces

So far luminance variations in a scene with uniform reflectance have been considered. Clearly if the various surfaces in the scene each had its own uniform reflectance that was different from the others, then the same argument would apply; but what if they were covered in texture?

Texture usually changes suddenly at surface discontinuities, but does not necessarily change at surface creases. Once again, we might invoke a device that was able to detect changes in texture and then apply the same argument looking for "texture discontinuities" or "texture gradient discontinuities".

The luminance approach discussed earlier worked well because it assumed that the changes in luminance in an image were all equally significant, although a problem with shadows was hinted at. But suppose that all the surfaces in Fig. 1.1 were covered in a texture of random grey markings, leading to a luminance profile such as that in Fig. 1.7. Now at the border between each black and white stripe, a luminance feature is produced that masquerades as a surface discontinuity, as can be seen from the second derivative below in the figure. It is easy to deduce that textured surfaces produce a further problem for the derived set of rules for using luminances.

It seems that we are left with the possibility that peaks in second derivatives of luminance waveforms do correspond to the important lines-of-sight that define surface shapes, but they also correspond to texture markings. However, there is another constraint that we can invoke to help with the texture problem. Texture markings are generally smaller in size than the surface they lie on: The average interval between luminance changes due to surface markings is much less than that due to surface changes. With this constraint, can we devise an operation that will suppress the texture in an image?

It is possible to replace the luminance value in an image by a local average luminance value. If the spatial distance over which the averaging is carried out is the same as or greater than the distance between texture markings, then these markings can be smoothed out. In general, it is preferable to use a weighted average, so that the nearest points have the largest effect and a large luminance change is kept relatively constrained in space. The process of smoothing is illustrated in Fig. 1.8.

Smoothing the image is a part solution to the problem. Figure 1.9 (top) shows the result of smoothing the textured image, and below is drawn the second derivative. Comparing this with the untextured original (see Fig. 1.3), it can be seen that smoothing has created distortions, and all the peaks in the

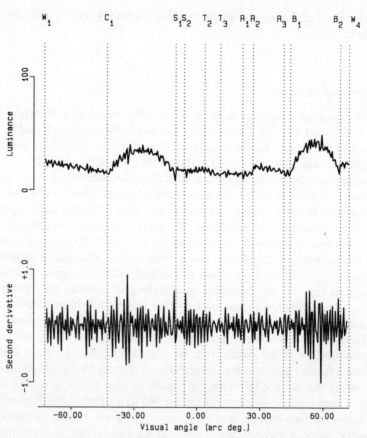

FIG. 1.7. This figure shows the luminance profile (top) and second derivative (bottom) of the scene image, as before, where all the surfaces are marked with a pattern of alternating light and dark texture elements. The points of special interest with respect to the original scene are now hidden in the second derivative signal by its response to the texture. The problem for the Primal Sketch now is to find the areas where, on the average or large spatial scale, luminance changes smoothly.

second derivative are much less sharp and also weaker; but nevertheless, some degree of success in finding surface features rather than texture markings has been achieved. In this instance, success is possible because the texture variations are small in size compared with the luminance variations of the untextured case, and of comparable amplitude. This may not always be the case, and smoothing is not invariably the solution.

The principle in this discussion of texture concerns the concept of *spatial scale*. We can define the term spatial scale as a measure of the distance over which averaging takes place for the process of smoothing. The spatial scale of smoothing that is sufficient to obliterate the texture depends on the texture,

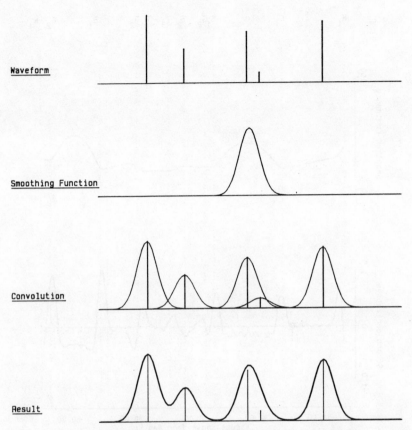

FIG. 1.8. Convolution is the process used to model the smoothing of an image by a smoothing function. At the top is shown an image comprising a few points (any number can be present and in the limit a continuous function is used). Below this is shown the smoothing function itself on the same scale. The third row shows one smoothing function per image element, placed at the position of that element and scaled in amplitude by the value of the element. The final row shows the result of adding together all the superimposed individual smoothing functions.

and cannot be known in advance. It is therefore necessary to be able to try different degrees of smoothing. Natural images are organised so that different types of information may co-exist at the same place in the image, but within different spatial scales. Smoothing has been introduced as a way of obliterating the finest scales, by averaging the luminance over the particular spatial scale.

Thus, two textured surfaces which are adjacent in the image and arranged so that they are each projecting the same luminance values for the black and white of their texture, can still be distinguished if the proportion of black to white varies between them, provided a spatial scale is selected at which the

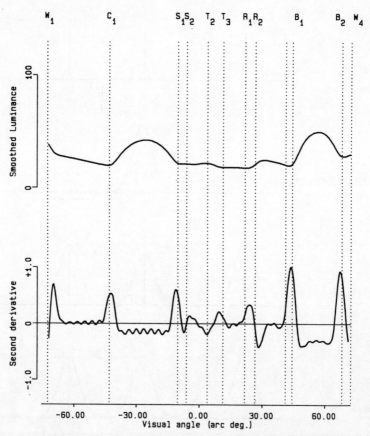

FIG. 1.9. This figure shows the result of smoothing the luminance waveform of Fig. 1.7 (top) and the second derivative of this smoothed luminance waveform (bottom). Note that the smoothing has largely removed the texture markings, but at the cost of loosing some of the accuracy in the placing of the points of special interest with respect to the original scene. The smoothing was done with a Gaussian function with a standard deviation of 1 arc degree.

texture is not resolved. At this spatial scale the two averaged grey-levels will be different, as can be seen in Fig. 1.10, and so this technique of smoothing can help to find texture differences as well as obliterate the texture elements themselves.

The concepts of spatial scale and smoothing are also helpful for dealing with shadows. The differences between the second derivative in Figs. 1.3 and 1.9 arise because all the luminance changes in the image are sudden. If a shadow were to be fairly blurred so that the luminance change was gradual, then there would be only a small difference between the second derivative and the smoothed second derivative. Smoothing provides a way of assessing

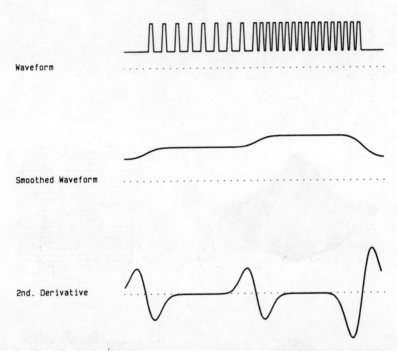

Texture 1.   Texture 2.

Waveform

Smoothed Waveform

2nd. Derivative

FIG. 1.10. This figure concerns two textures, differing only in the proportion of black and white. The top plot shows the two textures themselves. Below this is drawn a smoothed version of the waveform so that now the two different proportions of black and white become different grey-levels. In the bottom row is drawn the second derivative of the smoothed waveform. Note that the discontinuity between the two textures is now marked by a peak and a trough, but that these are themselves smooth.

the spatial scale of a luminance change, and any luminance change that is gradual is not likely to be due to a surface discontinuity or crease.

There is a difficulty in the use of smoothing. From the point of view of obliterating texture, the larger the scale of smoothing the better. From the point of view of preserving the occluding edges and creases of surfaces, the finer the scale the better. This means that in a given situation there will be an optimum degree of smoothing, but that this optimum will vary from surface to surface. Furthermore, the optimum may be a very poor optimum, suiting neither texture obliteration nor edge analysis. It is clearly necessary to use a range of different spatial scales, although this creates the new problem of how to combine the information at different scales. I shall return to this later.

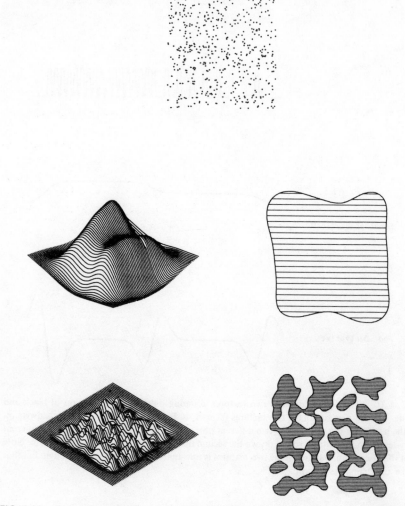

FIG. 1.11.   A two-dimensional texture at the top. Below this is shown the response of a large filter (middle) and a small filter (bottom). Notice that the large filter eradicates the texture.

TWO DIMENSIONS

We must briefly consider how far this discussion can be extended to two dimensions without loss of generality.

The first point to note is that the direction or orientation of surface contours is not constrained, except by the slight preponderance of verticals and horizontals in most scenes arising from the horizon and most man-made

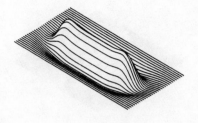

FIG. 1.12.   The response of an isotropic filter to an elongated line.

structures. As a result of this lack of constraint, it is necessary to take second derivatives in all directions in the image. This can be accomplished algebraically by differentiating (taking a derivative) twice horizontally and twice vertically. These two operations can be combined into a single one called the Laplacian and denoted by the symbol ∇^2 (pronounced del-squared):

Image: I

differentiate twice horizontally: $\dfrac{d^2I}{dx^2}$

differentiate twice vertically: $\dfrac{d^2I}{dy^2}$

Their sum: $\dfrac{d^2I}{dx^2} + \dfrac{d^2I}{dy^2}$

is equivalent to $\nabla^2 I.$

This is the argument of Marr and Hildreth (1980) who discuss alternatives.

How does the response of these filters in two dimensions relate to the one-dimensional case just discussed?

First, smoothing in two dimensions will eradicate texture just as it did in one dimension. See Fig. 1.11.

Second, where there are elongated and smoothly curved creases or occluding edges, there will be elongated ridges and valleys in the two-

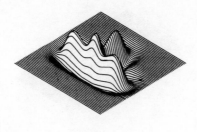

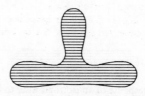

FIG. 1.13.   The response of an isotropic filter to a T intersection of lines.

dimensional response in place of the one-dimensional peak/troughs. See Fig. 1.12.

Third, where there are corners and intersections in creases and/or occluding edges, there are discrete peaks, i.e. real summits, and pits in the two-dimensional second derivative. This is because at these points, the luminance is changing in more than one direction. The total change, summed around the clock, is thus greater at a corner than it is along an elongated edge. See Fig. 1.13.

Figure 1.14 shows a two-dimensional view of the scene of Fig. 1.1, as it would appear to an observer at the point O. This view is an abstraction because it contains no texture or shading. It can be considered as an ideal outcome of applying smoothing to remove the texture and noise, and then applying an edge-finder to locate just the surface creases and occluding edges. The figure shows that all of these features can be regarded as either elongated contours (i.e. edges or creases) or contour intersections.

There are three points to make with regard to this distinction between elongated contours and intersections. First, the intersections are all points of particularly high importance for the reconstruction or analysis of the scene. Second, they are selectively detected by the Laplacian operator, that is, by differentiating in two dimensions. Third, the elongated contours are not much affected by smoothing, whereas the intersections are obviously blurred.

Thus, when the analysis is extended to two dimensions, there are two

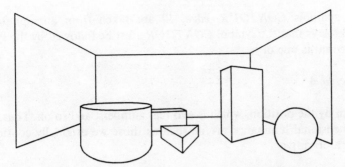

FIG. 1.14.   This figure shows a two-dimensional edge-map representation of the imaginary scene from Fig. 1.1. Note that the perspective appears distorted because the image covers a wide horizontal angle (150 degrees); but of course, this diagram does not itself cover the same visual angle. The image is made up of elongated contours that are oriented at all angles, and contour intersections.

categories of features that should be sought. There are the smoothly elongated contours and the intersections. It is very helpful to find that the Laplacian, which is a two-dimensional extension to the idea of a second derivative, not only finds these two classes of features, but also marks them with a slightly different feature: Intersections are marked by summits/pits; elongated contours are marked by ridges/valleys.

THE NATURE OF THE REPRESENTATION

What is a representation? A representation is a device for producing a description of a particular image. This definition follows Marr (1976). The description is based on an *alphabet* of *symbols* and a *grammar* of *primitives* or rules for combining the symbols to create the *sentences* of a *description*.

We can actually write these sentences down on paper, although they will look a little strange. I shall follow the convention employed in Set Theory and use the curly brackets "{" and "}" when the order of the items between is irrelevant. The angular brackets "⟨" and "⟩" refer to a list of items whose order is important, so that the position of any particular item in a list has meaning derived from what it is, and where it is. Normal brackets "(" and ")" enclose co-ordinate pairs that are actually one item. For example, take the representational sentence:

⟨CONTOUR: edge; (0,0); 10; 90⟩.

This might be a way of saying: "There is a contour in the image; it is an edge; it is at position (0,0); it has a length of 10; it has an orientation of 90."

The symbols *CONTOUR, edge, 10* are taken from an alphabet. A grammar says that the symbol *CONTOUR* must be followed by the type of contour that is one of:

{*edge, line*}

and then by the position, which is two real numbers, and so on. Thus, for a one-dimensional luminance profile such as those we originally considered, there is a primitive:

⟨CONTOUR: type; position; length; orientation⟩

that will describe any one image feature. The full description will then be a set of sentences based on this primitive form. Take the tall rectangle on the right of the scene in Fig. 1.14. This can be represented by a set of ⟨CONTOUR⟩ sentences. This is illustrated in Fig. 1.15. Note that this representation is *complete* in that the line drawing can be reconstructed in its entirety from the description given. However, the representation would not be *sufficient* if you were asked to touch the nearest corner of the rectangle. A second

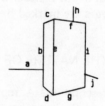

<START	:	TYPE	:	POSITION	:	LENGTH	:	ORIENTATION	: >
<CONTOUR a :	edge	:	(15, −9)	:	16	:	0	: >
<CONTOUR b :	edge	:	(21, −2)	:	28	:	90	: >
<CONTOUR c :	edge	:	(24, 13)	:	5	:	21	: >
<CONTOUR d :	edge	:	(24, −18)	:	6	:	−39	: >
<CONTOUR e :	edge	:	(26, −1)	:	33	:	90	: >
<CONTOUR f :	edge	:	(34, 13)	:	14	:	−8	: >
<CONTOUR g :	edge	:	(33, −18)	:	15	:	16	: >
<CONTOUR h :	edge	:	(36, 16)	:	8	:	90	: >
<CONTOUR i :	edge	:	(41, −2)	:	28	:	90	: >
<CONTOUR j :	edge	:	(44, −12)	:	7	:	−19	: >

<END.>

FIG. 1.15. This figure shows a part of the scene in Fig. 1.14 and its description according to the simple representation scheme outlined in the text.

representation that made the location of the corner *explicit* would be needed because the presence of corners is only *implicit* in the ⟨CONTOUR⟩ representation.

We have already seen in the discussion of two dimensions that it would be possible to detect corners and intersections directly in the image, rather than calculating where lines intersect. Therefore, we introduce a second representational sentence primitive:

⟨INTERSECTION: type; position; direction(s):⟩

where type is one of:

{*one-way*, *two-way*, *three-way*}.

Figure 1.16 shows the same portion of the scene, with a set of sentences using the ⟨INTERSECTION⟩ primitive. Note that this representation is also complete, but is not necessarily sufficient for all tasks.

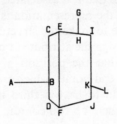

```
<START           :  TYPE :  POSITION  ;  DIRECTIONS  :>

<INTERSECTION A :   one  ; (  6, -11) ;    0           :>
<INTERSECTION B : three  ; ( 22, -11) ;    0,  90, -90 :>
<INTERSECTION C :   two  ; ( 22,   9) ; -90,  21       :>
<INTERSECTION D :   two  ; ( 22, -19) ;   90, -39      :>
<INTERSECTION E : three  ; ( 27,  11) ;   21,  -8, -90 :>
<INTERSECTION F : three  ; ( 27, -22) ;   90,  16, -39 :>
<INTERSECTION G :   one  ; ( 36,  17) ;  -90           :>
<INTERSECTION H : three  ; ( 36,  10) ;   90, -82,  -8 :>
<INTERSECTION I :   two  ; ( 41,   9) ;  -82, -90      :>
<INTERSECTION J :   two  ; ( 41, -19) ;   90,  16      :>
<INTERSECTION K : three  ; ( 41, -13) ;   90, -19, -90 :>
<INTERSECTION L :   one  ; ( 47, -15) ;  -71           :>

<END.>
```

FIG. 1.16.   This figure shows a part of the scene in Fig. 1.14 and its description according to the simple representation scheme outlined in the text.

There are two sets of sentences describing the image. It is valid to form a third representation by taking the union of these two sets, that is, by taking the two together. This representation is also complete, and it is obviously sufficient for a wider range of tasks. This representation is *redundant* because it contains more sentences than are strictly necessary.

The representation of an image thus comprises a set of sentences. All the members of such sets have equal status, but we can refine the representation concept to allow the creation of hierarchical structure within a description. Consider how the ⟨INTERSECTION⟩ and ⟨CONTOUR⟩ primitives differ in their logic.

An intersection is a place where two or more contours are connected to each other; a contour is a connection between two intersections. This means that we could add a further piece of information into the two primitives. Suppose that each of the sentences in the description was uniquely labelled with a name, as they are in Figs. 1.15 and 1.16. It is then possible for each ⟨INTERSECTION⟩ sentence to list the names of the ⟨CONTOUR⟩ sentences that describe these contours meeting at that particular intersection. Similarly each ⟨CONTOUR⟩ sentence could list the two ⟨INTERSECT-ION⟩ sentences that it is associated with. We now have sentences *pointing* to sentences, and the representation is beginning to assume a structure.

It is possible to make the structure hierarchical. A simple way to do this would be to assign the attribute of position only to the ⟨INTERSECTION⟩ primitive, so that the position of a contour is represented only by the identities of its end-points, which are intersections. Within this framework, it would be useful to have a third list of the spatial relationships between intersections where no real contour exists:

⟨IMAGINARY CONTOUR: length; orientation⟩.

With this added to the alphabet, it would be possible to dispense with the attribute of position completely because there would be a complete representation of all spatial relationships. This would be sensible because position in a two-dimensional image plane is not meaningful, except as a way of obtaining spatial relationships, which can then replace it.

The grammar of the representation can be refined a little more by organising the two sets of ⟨CONTOUR⟩ and ⟨IMAGINARY CON-TOUR⟩ into one structure, a set of ⟨CONTOUR⟩ sentences that can be of three types: *edge*, *line*, and *imaginary*.

How does this type of representation help the vision process? The answer to this question has two parts. First, interesting and relevant features of the image are represented somewhere in it, by design. Second, we can look at the hierarchy to see how it affects the accessibility of those features. The most accessible parts of the representation are the list of corners and the list of connections, which between them and without reference to their attributes provide a topological representation. For many perceptual processes this topological representation will provide much of the necessary information. Much of a body's three-dimensional structure can be inferred from a list of sharp corners in its image and their relations—which is connected to which. Reading text is a process where a list of line intersections and their topological relations will generally aid considerably in identifying letters and words by restricting the set of possibilities. Of course, the finer geometric information, particularly concerning the shape of the extant connections, is also available and useful.

Other properties of the image are also represented. For example, by noting which connections are real, it is possible to deduce properties such as closure of a chain of contours. The information necessary to construct a position, in some arbitrary metric, for each intersection is available, even if the representation is only in terms of the length and orientation of each connection.

SUMMARY

In these introductory remarks, the goal of Primal Sketch visual processing has been defined as a representation of all the boundaries in the image between different smooth surfaces, and a representation of the reflectance characteristics of these surfaces. This is really only possible because there are constraints on the way in which images are formed, and several such constraints have been explored.

The first constraint that has been exploited concerns the manner in which luminance varies in images. Sudden changes (discontinuities) in luminance or luminance gradient can often be attributed to surface discontinuities and creases because the reflector on surfaces usually changes little. The sudden changes in luminance or its gradient are due to sudden changes in surface reflectance, range, or orientation, usually corresponding to points of interest in the scene. In order to find discontinuities in luminance and luminance gradient, it is necessary to differentiate the image twice and look for peaks. Shadows and texture can also give rise to these features, however, and the method is far from ideal.

A second constraint was used to help with texture. It was noted that texture markings are generally smaller than the surfaces they lie on. This allows the use of smoothing to find some of the underlying surface structure, although the distance or spatial scale of smoothing has to be chosen intelligently by the processing system.

A bonus obtained from using the second derivative of the image was found to be the prominence accorded to corners and intersections. The consequences that follow from this for the language of the representation were explored, and it was found that a natural outcome is a structured grammar.

THE FIRST PROBLEM

There is one difficulty with the argument so far. We have identified the need for the *intelligent* use of smoothing, that is, for second derivative analysis at various spatial scales. How is the information from these different spatial scales to be selected or combined? This question is addressed in the next chapter of this essay.

2 A Model for the Primal Sketch

Watt and Morgan (1984, 1985) have proposed a model for the early stages of visual processing that describes how the outputs of differently sized spatial filters could be combined and then analysed to produce a symbolic description of the image. The model, MIRAGE, accounts for a considerable range of data with a relatively small number of free parameters. A full understanding of any visual process must involve a model of that process and a theory of how that model generally relates to the behaviour of seeing. This second half is what Marr (1982) termed the computational theory level of explanation: What is being computed by a process and why. In the sections that follow, some answers to this computational question for MIRAGE will be examined, but the model itself will be described first of all, followed by a review of the evidence that supports the various steps.

The MIRAGE model relates closely to the arguments of the preceding chapter. It starts with the image luminance waveform, which it smooths to a variety of extents, and then takes the second derivative of each of the smoothed images independently. The resultant functions are examined for features that correspond to the isolated peaks and troughs. Finally, the sequence of these is examined to determine whether a luminance discontinuity or luminance gradient discontinuity (edge or line) is responsible.

SPATIAL FILTERS

The two operations of differentiating an image and smoothing an image have been introduced in the first chapter of this essay as ways of: (1) revealing

27

discontinuities in luminance and luminance gradient; and (2) hiding fine texture detail. It is a property of the algebra of these two processes that they can be combined into one operation. In smoothing the luminance values of the image, a new image is built by replacing every point in the image by a smoothing function centred at that point and scaled in height to the luminance value in the image at that point. The result is a series of partially overlapping smoothing functions, one at every point in the image. The value at a given point in the new smoothed image is thus the sum of a set of values, one contributed by every smoothing function and determined by the amplitude and distance of the given point away from the centre of that function. The smoothing function can be of any form; the process uses a mathematical operation known as *convolution* and was illustrated in Fig. 1.8. A useful property of convolutions is that like additions they are commutative; if several convolutions are to be done, the order in which they are performed does not matter. The next point is that differentiation can be executed by a convolution. Thus in taking second derivatives and smoothing images, we are really convolving together four functions: the smoothing function, the differentiation function twice, and the image. The first three of these can be combined to produce a composite function, the second derivative of the smoothing filter, which can then be convolved with the image. This is shown in Fig. 2.1. This composite function is called a *spatial filter*, and we shall be much concerned with the properties of spatial filters. Indeed, the introduction to this essay could have been described in terms of spatial filters. Filters that are expressed by convolution are said to be linear. This means that their response to the sum of two inputs is the same as the sum of their responses to each input separately:

$$R(A + B) = R(A) + R(B)$$

where A, B are two input patterns and $R(A)$ is the filter response to A.

Gaussian Filters

There is a particular class of spatial filter that has two very useful properties. The filters concerned are the Gaussian function and its derivatives. This is the same as the bell-shaped normal distribution. The first property is that when a Gaussian is convolved with a second Gaussian the result is also a Gaussian with a variance equal to the sum of the two contributory Gaussians. When a Gaussian is convolved with itself, a Gaussian wider by a factor of $2^{\frac{1}{2}}$ is produced.

The second property is concerned with the effects of the size of the Gaussian on the structure of the new image. A fundamental result of mathematics, the diffusion equation, shows that as the size of the Gaussian is

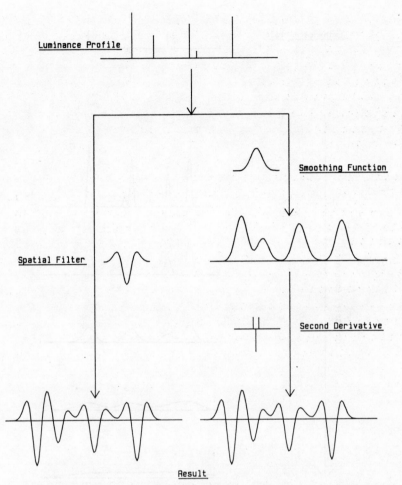

FIG. 2.1. Convolution is commutative, which means that the two operations of differentiating twice and smoothing can be combined into the single operation of convolution with the second derivative of the smoothing function, as illustrated by the figure.

gradually and continuously increased, the number of peaks and troughs in the convolution output can only be reduced: The peaks tend to merge together. The things that cannot happen are the appearance of a new peak and the splitting of one extant peak into two. This is of course why smoothing helped with the texture problem of Chapter 1, and it allows us to be confident that the number of peaks and troughs will be roughly in inverse proportion to the size of the spatial filter. The mathematics of this will be found in Koenderink (1984). Figure 2.2 illustrates this behaviour with

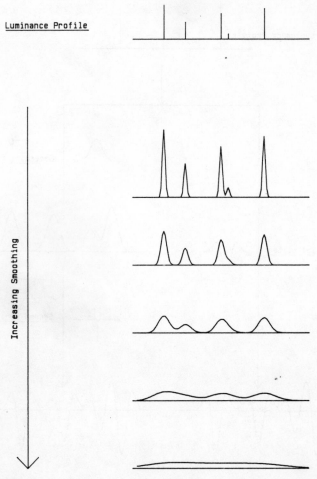

FIG. 2.2.   This shows the effect of increasing the spatial extent of smoothing on an arbitrary luminance profile.

increasing smoothing. Notice that moving down the figure, as the distance of smoothing increases, the amount of detail decreases.

A two-dimensional Gaussian of space constant f is easiest described in polar co-ordinates; where r is the distance from the centre of the Gaussian, and θ is the direction:

$$G(r, \theta, f) = e^{-r^2/2f^2}.$$

This equation is simply the standard Gaussian function from one dimension, with the space constant f, equivalent to the standard deviation of the normal distribution. Polar co-ordinates specify a direction θ from the centre and a distance r. In this case θ is irrelevant: It does not appear on the right-hand side of the equation and the Gaussian is circularly symmetric. The maximum amplitude of this function has a value of unity (at $r = 0$).

Laplacian of a Gaussian Filter

There is one particular Gaussian filter that is important, and that will be used exclusively in the model to follow: The Laplacian of a Gaussian. The Laplacian of a Gaussian, $\nabla^2 G$ (del-squared g) is given by:

$$\nabla^2 G(r, \theta, f) = \left(1 - \frac{r^2}{2f^2} \right) e^{-r^2/2f^2}.$$

Once again this is given in a form where the maximum amplitude (at $r = 0$) is unity. The Laplacian of a Gaussian is shown in Fig. 2.3.

This particular filter is important for vision for several reasons. It has two simple algebraic properties. If one were to integrate this filter function over the whole (r, θ) plane, then the sum obtained is zero: The filter is *balanced*

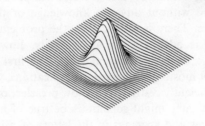

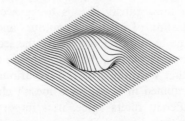

FIG. 2.3.   The top of this figure shows a Laplacian of a Gaussian filter; the bottom of the figure shows the same filter but negated.

between positive and negative values. This means that the filter output is at zero over an area of the image where luminance does not change and the mean luminance of the entire image is not registered in the filter output. It also means that the response to a light/dark edge is exactly opposite to the response to a dark/light edge. The filter expression does not refer to the co-ordinate θ: The filter is said to be *isotropic*, or circularly symmetric. The filter does not prefer edges or lines of any particular orientation.

THE MIRAGE ALGORITHM

In the first chapter of this essay, the discussion centred on the *operations* of differentiation and smoothing, the *analysis* of the resultant functions to find peaks/troughs, and finally the *interpretation* of the sequence of peaks to determine whether they were caused by lines or edges. The MIRAGE algorithm has the same three parts.

The Theory behind MIRAGE

The reason for having a range of sizes of filters was principally to allow the smoothing of texture without advance knowledge of the exact form or density of the texture. There is immediately the problem of how either to select the size that is adequate, or alternatively, how to combine the information from the filters of different sizes. The first alternative is the choice in many, if not most, machine-vision applications, where the range of images is usually sufficiently restricted to allow preselection of the appropri-ate size of filter. The same might sometimes be true of human vision. The range of different sizes and spacings in the letters of printed text is really rather small, and it is at least plausible that an intelligent visual system could predict a particular filter size for the special task of reading. However, more generally, high-level knowledge is unlikely to be able to predict reliably the appropriate scale of analysis before it has started that analysis.

Therefore, the alternative approach of combining the filter outputs in some way has to be explored. We can start by specifying some conditions that the combination must satisfy if it is to be acceptable. Recall that detection and identification of occluding contours and creases, edges and lines, were done on the basis of regions where the second derivative filter outputs departed from zero. It was the sign of these departures and their spatial arrangement that were important. The various sized filter outputs must therefore be combined in a way that doesn't change these response properties. Where different filters agree, it is important to register and emphasise this. Where they disagree, it is important also to register this.

Under some circumstances, simply adding the response functions together

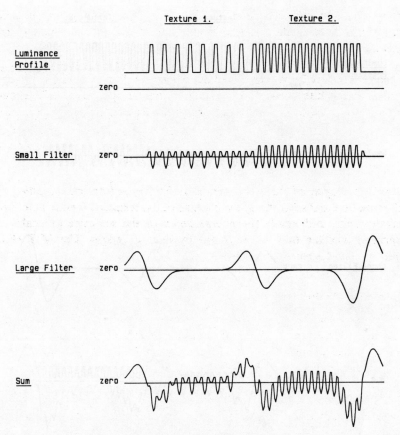

FIG. 2.4. A pair of textures are illustrated along with the responses of a small and a large filter. The sum of the two filter outputs is shown on the bottom row.

would meet this criterion. For example, if the texture caused luminance variations that were lower in amplitude (and second derivative response) than the contour luminance variations, then the negative portions of the fine spatial scale responses would be too near zero to pull the superimposed positive portions at the larger scales down below zero. This is shown in Fig. 2.4.

This cannot be relied on, and might even be the exception rather than the rule. Even so, this consideration has shown that the problem with such a suggestion is that just adding the responses together may not preserve the sign of the larger filter's response. This problem can be resolved very easily: Add the fine-scale response to the large-scale response only where they have the same sign. In other words, take each filter response and split it into two responses, one only positive or zero, the other only negative or zero. This is

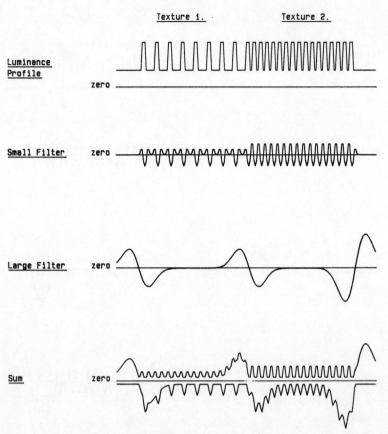

FIG. 2.5. This is the same as Fig. 2.4, except that the filter outputs are split into positive and negative before being summed, positive with positive and negative with negative.

shown in Fig. 2.5. All the positive responses can then be added together, and all the negative responses can also be added together, but separately from the positive ones. This is the MIRAGE operation.

Let me emphasise this double point. The sign of the filter responses is crucial and to be preserved. This is why the responses are initially split according to sign. Where filters have the same sign, their responses can be combined. Addition is suitable, a logical OR might do; multiplication and a logical AND would not do.

The MIRAGE Operation

For an illustration of the MIRAGE transformation, please inspect Fig. 2.6 while reading this part of the text. At the top of the figure is a stimulus luminance profile.

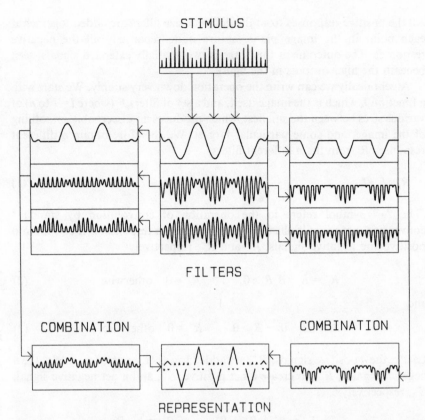

FIG. 2.6.   An illustration of the action of MIRAGE. At the top is shown a stimulus, and beneath it the responses of three different scale filters are stacked with the largest at the top. Three are chosen just for graphical convenience. These responses are then split into their positive portions and their negative portions, shown on the left and right of the filter responses. All the positive signals are added together, as are all the negative signals. The resultant S signals are then analysed in terms of the central moments of their zero-bounded response distributions.

MIRAGE starts with a set of spatial filters, of various sizes, each of which is independently convolved with the retinal image as can be seen in the three panels beneath the stimulus in the figure. The exact nature of the filters is not important: They are presumed to have balanced positive and negative weighted inputs in a circularly symmetric centre-surround arrangement. The Laplacian of a Gaussian, $\nabla^2 G(f)$, is taken as a standard form, where f is the (standard deviation) space constant of the filter. The convolutions are each split into a positive portion and a negative portion: This is equivalent to having a positive or on-centre and a separate negative or off-centre filter and half-wave rectifying the output of each. In the figure these are drawn left and right of the filter outputs.

The important step is the next step where the filter outputs are combined.

All the positive responses from the different size filters are added together at each point in the image plane, as are quite separately all the negative responses. The outcome at this stage is two spatially extended signals, seen beneath the filter outputs in the figure.

Algebraically we can write the operation down very simply. We start with a function I, which is the image itself, and a set of filters F_i (where $i = 1$ to n) of various sizes between the smallest, which produces no discernable smoothing of the image, and some particular largest. We therefore obtain n different responses R_i from the n different filters,

$$R_i = F_i * I \qquad (1)$$

(The "$*$" symbol refers to the operation of convolution by standard convention, not to multiplication!) Each of these n responses is then split into positive and negative signals, R_i^+ and R_i^-, respectively:

$$R_i^+ = R_i \quad \text{if } R_i > 0, \qquad R_i^+ = 0 \quad \text{otherwise} \qquad (2)$$

and

$$R_i^- = R_i \quad \text{if } -R_i > 0, \qquad R_i^- = 0 \quad \text{otherwise.} \qquad (2)$$

Lastly, the n positive signals, R_i^+, are added together, as are, separately, the n negative signals, R_i^-, to create a net positive, S^+, and a net negative signal, S^-, respectively:[1]

$$S_i^+ = R_1^+ + R_2^+ + R_3^+ \ldots + R_n^+ = \sum_{i=1}^{n} R_i^+ \qquad (3)$$

and

$$S_i^- = R_1^- + R_2^- + R_3^- \ldots + R_n^- = \sum_{i=1}^{n} R_i^- \qquad (3)$$

The only three free parameters of this algorithm are the sizes of the smallest and largest filters and the size ratio of adjacent sizes. The smallest filter is matched to the resolution acuity limit of the visual system (it has a space constant of 0.35 arc min). The size of the largest filter will be discussed later and is left for the present as the only important free parameter.

So far this algorithm works strictly in the image plane: In each case the domain and co-domain (input and output) of steps (1) to (3) is just the set of real numbers over the area of the image, the x-dimension and the

---

[1] Watt and Morgan (1985) originally referred to the S signals as the T signals. I have changed this terminology to bring it into agreement with that used by Marr and Ullman (1981).

y-dimension. These three steps will be called the MIRAGE operation, which takes an image, I, and for a given setting of the parameter n produces two output functions, S^+ and S^-. The important details of this operation are two-fold. First, step (2), which splits the filter convolution outputs into two separate functions according to the sign of the output, is critical for most of what follows. Second, step (3), which combines all the filters together, is also important. At the end of step (2), the one image function has been replaced by $2n$ response functions. Step (3) collapses these down into just two functions, which, as will be elaborated later, are carrying different information at most points in the image plane. The combination of the filter outputs is taken as an addition, but it could be one of many others, with similar behaviour. Addition is the simplest and is particularly useful in keeping noise down.

The first three rows of Fig. 2.7 show the effect of applying the MIRAGE operation to the luminance image of the scene with texture taken from Fig. 1.7. The fourth row is concerned with analysis and will be considered later. At the top is drawn the luminance profile itself. Beneath this, in the second row, are drawn a selection of filter outputs obtained with filters of various sizes. The smoothest functions come from the largest filters. In the third row are the two signals, S^+ and S^-; a convention is used at this stage so that the two are vertically separated for clarity. Much will be made of the properties of MIRAGE in the chapters that follow, but for the present it is worth noting that in Fig. 2.7 it has sorted out the various luminance changes into overall structure and finest detail.

Considered simply as a modification of the original image, perhaps with a view to reducing its information content (in absolute terms), there are several interesting aspects. Images generally pose two difficulties for machinery. First, the range of luminance values can be enormous, even within a single scene, although important scene details may give rise to small differences in luminance at the same time. The second problem is that photon noise is always present in an image, and it is higher the greater the luminance level. Any code for an image has thus to cope with the competing requirements of a large dynamic range and high-differential sensitivity in the presence of noise.

An important characteristic of balanced linear filters is their zero response to the mean level of luminance: They are responsive only to spatial differences in luminance. The Laplacian second derivative filters are in addition insensitive to linear changes in luminance. As a consequence, the largest effects of general illumination strength and direction are not passed through the initial stages, although secondary consequences in contrast range and photon noise are. The image is subject to *photon noise*, simply as a property of light, and the amplitude of this photon noise rises with mean luminance (actually in proportion to its square root). There is also, however, *intrinsic noise* within the visual system, which may be thought of as noise

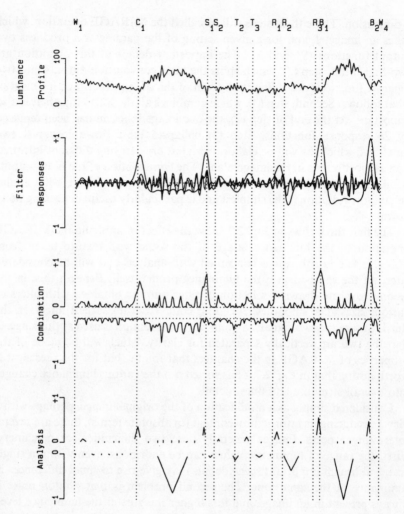

FIG. 2.7. The top of this figure shows the luminance profile of Fig. 1.7. The rest of the figure illustrates MIRAGE in action upon that profile. Notice that both the texture and some scene features are preserved.

added to the filter outputs, R_i. A low gain in the filters unfortunately decreases the signal-to-noise ratio when this intrinsic noise is dominant. However, there is a step in the MIRAGE operation that reduces the intrinsic noise. By adding the various filter responses together, any intrinsic noise that is not correlated between the filters is reduced with respect to the signal. In the next section we shall see that the goal of reducing the effects of this intrinsic noise is important in determining how the output of the MIRAGE operation is to be analysed.

The output of the MIRAGE operation is not strictly a representation: It is not a description of the image; it is merely two new functions that are related to the original image in a manner defined by equations (1) to (3) but have not yet been described in terms of their effect or function. It is called an *operation* because the *co-domain* (output) and *domain* (input) of the process have the same dimensions. The operation is to be followed by an *analysis* of the signals S^+ and S^-, followed in turn by an *interpretation* of what is found, so that a representation of the original image can be created.

The MIRAGE analysis

The MIRAGE analysis step can be thought of as a means of producing a code of the signals S^+, S^- in a form that makes the final interpretation in symbolic terms straightforward.

These S signals are rather unusual, and it is worth describing them first. In the presence of a uniform field of luminance, they are both at zero. If there are variations in luminance, then either or both will depart from zero. The S^+ signal will always be either zero or positive; the S^- signal will always be either zero or negative. Where there is a change in the rate of luminance change in the image, the S signals will be non-zero over a reasonable distance: There will be a broad distribution of response away from zero. In general, these S signals can be thought of as being made up of areas of zero-response, and distributions of response that are bounded by zero-response. These will be called *zero-bounded response distributions*.

The analysis scheme that Watt and Morgan proposed was that each signal, S^+ and S^-, was quite separately broken down into a sequence of zero-bounded response distributions and regions of zero-response. There are many ways in which a distribution can be characterised. Watt and Morgan proposed the use of the statistical *central moments* of centroid (mean), mass, and standard deviation. These are the most reliable measures of where a distribution is, how large it is, and how broad it is, respectively, when the exact form of the distribution is unknown or variable. The fourth row of Fig. 2.7 shows the various zero-bounded distributions graphically drawn as a sequence of chevrons. By convention the height of each chevron marks the mass of the corresponding distribution; the position of the apex marks the location of its centroid; and the base width of the chevron is set to twice the standard deviation.

In understanding the reasons for this particular form of analysis, we may enquire how the S signals are constrained. All the figures showing second derivatives, or filter responses, or two S signals illustrate the fact that such responses are constrained to have an expected mean value of zero; in other words, positive values are as likely as negative values. Yet a further way of expressing this is to say that surface creases in an image are equally as likely to be concave as convex, with respect to the observer, and that surface discontinuities are equally as likely to be on the left of objects as the right. It is these deviations from the mean value that should be analysed, preserving their sign.

A second constraint that helps in understanding how the signals are to be analysed is to note that *both* signals will tend to be at zero where there are surfaces that tend to be imaged as areas where luminance or luminance gradient does not change. If the image were all just random noise, then occasions when *both* signals were at zero at the same place in space would be very rare. The occurrence of places where both signals are at zero is a significant event, and so the analysis of S^+ and S^- should distinguish regions of response from regions of no response.

In real operating conditions, noise (photon and intrinsic) is a factor to be considered. Noise in the filter responses, prior to the separation of positive and negative regions, will cause the S^+ signal to be at rest at a value, $+s$, a little above zero, and S^- at a value, $-s$, a little below zero. The reason for this is that, although the noise in the filter responses has a mean value of zero, when all the negative values are set to zero to create S^+, in step (2) of the MIRAGE transformation, all the noise values, and so also the mean noise level, become zero or positive. It is s-bounded distributions rather than zero-bounded distributions that should be analysed. Noise also reduces the accuracy with which the S signals can be analysed, although it affects the central moments much less than it would affect, for example, peaks, or zero-crossings. It is worth noting that intrinsic noise actually has a positive advantage, in that it will truncate the shallow tails of response distributions. This can be seen in Fig. 2.8, which shows a typical filter response with low and high noise. The more noise there is the smaller the spatial extent of the zero-bounded response distribution in the signal, because the higher amplitude noise cuts the gradual tails off the distribution.

In the absence of any luminance changes in the image there will be a large number of zero-bounded distributions due solely to intrinsic noise. These will all have small values for their mass, and the distribution of such masses will be determined by the noise amplitude and the density at which the image is sampled. This distribution can be regarded as a relatively fixed property of the system, and so it is possible for zero-bounded distributions generated only by noise to be removed by examining the mass of each distribution found in the signals S^+ and S^- and comparing it with a threshold determined *a priori* from the noise distribution. This removal of the parts of S^+ and S^- caused by noise is important, because the interpretation of the sequence of distributions depends on correctly identifying those regions where the signal is at zero.

The S signals are analysed into a sequence of zero-bounded distributions of response activity and zero-response regions. The distributions are then

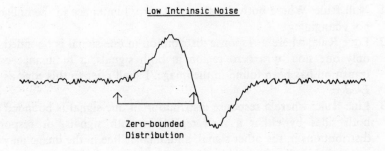

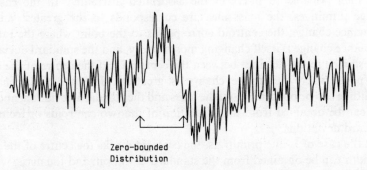

FIG. 2.8.   This figure illustrates how intrinsic noise can be useful in truncating the ends of zero-bounded distributions of response. At the top, the level of noise is low and the distribution is larger in spatial spread than the distribution in the response at the bottom, where there is a high level of intrinsic noise.

characterised by their central moments, and several reasons for this have been discussed. In the next section the interpretation of the sequence will be discussed.

The MIRAGE Interpretation

Watt and Morgan described how, in one dimension, the zero-valued regions of these signals and the zero-bounded response distributions can be examined to determine whether they are to be attributed to an edge or a line. Recall that these terms were introduced on p. 11 ff. The decision is determined by the spatial sequence of the loci of zero-values in both signals and response distributions in either signal. Three interpretative rules are employed:

1. Null Rule: Where both signals are at zero, luminance in the image is not changing.
2. Edge Rule: where a response distribution in one signal is bounded on only one side by a zero region in both signals, a luminance edge transition has been found in the image. I shall refer to this edge as an *L-edge*.
3. Line Rule: where a response distribution in one signal is bounded on both sides by either a zero region in both signals, or response distributions in the other signal, a luminance line in the image may be inferred. I shall refer to this as an *L-line*.

After these rules have been used to identify the type of primitive involved, it is then possible to interpret the associated attributes. In the case of L-edge primitives, the mass measure corresponds to the greatest rate of luminance change; the centroid corresponds to the point where the rate of luminance change is itself changing most rapidly; and the standard deviation corresponds to the distance between the centroid and the centre of the edge (the point where luminance change is greatest). The luminance change amplitude can be obtained from the mass and the standard deviation, and the blur can be obtained from the separation of the two centroids or from the standard deviations.

In the case of L-line primitives, the centroid marks the centre of the line; its width can be obtained from the standard deviation; and the mass, which itself is a measure of the change in the rate of luminance change at the crease, when multiplied by the standard deviation gives the luminance amplitude.

SOME OF THE EVIDENCE CONCERNING MIRAGE

This exposition of the MIRAGE model has been conducted as an abstract exercise, the only justification offered at any point in this essay so far being strictly computational. The logic has been to make assertions about the general structure of scenes and images and then to derive implications for models of the Primal Sketch. In this section, some of the psychophysical evidence concerning MIRAGE will be described.

The evidence to be presented is not the complete set; I have selected the most important or interesting items that force the conclusions leading to steps (1) to (3) of the MIRAGE transformation and the MIRAGE analysis and interpretation. The account is not historical either: In retrospect it is often the case that the first demonstration of a particular type of behaviour can be seen as clumsy. A much wider range of experimental evidence relating to the computational aspects of MIRAGE will be dispersed throughout later chapters of this essay.

The difficulty in interpreting psychophysical data is that subjects' responses are based on descriptions of the stimuli which may only indirectly reflect the processes that created the representation. The factors that limit psychophysical performance include: photon noise (not very important), spatial filter sensitivity and intrinsic noise, positional uncertainty or error in mapping through steps (1) to (3), the algorithm itself, and psychological decision factors.

The account of the evidence that follows is rather technical in a number of places. These technicalities are presented so that the interested reader can examine them and see the nature of psychophysical hypotheses and data. It is, however, possible for the non-technically minded reader to use Figs. 2.9 to 2.16 to form an impression of the quality of the data and skip the technical arguments in the text.

Independent Filters

The evidence for step (1), the spatial filters, is particularly difficult to assess because the filters themselves are linear operators, which means they preserve information. There are two broad sources of experimental data and each requires additional assumptions to be made for it to be interpreted.

The original experiments were conceived in terms of the *spatial frequency* of repetitive or periodic patterns of long parallel light and dark stripes. The spatial frequency of such a pattern is the number of repetitions per degree of visual angle (cycles per degree, c/deg). These patterns are useful because when the luminance variation is a sine-wave they will interest a smaller range of different sized filters than any other pattern.

The first observation to make about such *sine-wave grating* patterns is that the luminance contrast between the light and dark bars that is needed for the pattern to be just visible depends on the spatial frequency of the grating (Campbell & Robson, 1968). This is shown in Figure 2.9, which also shows as a continuous heavy line the MIRAGE model. This prediction is not critical because the range of filters could be adjusted to fit the data. The next finding is that the contrast threshold for other types of periodic patterns can be predicted from this set of data. For a range of different patterns that can be made by superimposing various sine-wave gratings of differing spatial frequencies, the contrast threshold is determined by the single frequency that reaches its own threshold first. There is no measurable advantage gained from having other frequencies present (Campbell & Robson, 1968), although this is now known to be over-simplified (Pelli, 1985). The conclusion reached was that different spatial frequencies are detected independently, presumably by mechanisms that are selective for a narrow range of spatial frequencies.

If the stimulus pattern contains, in addition to the test grating that is to be detected, a second grating of different spatial frequency, then the contrast

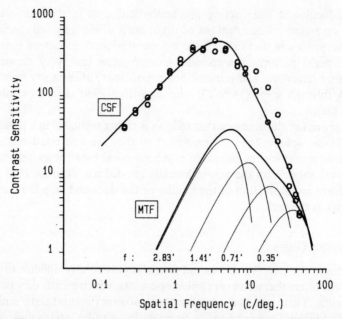

FIG. 2.9. The data points show how sensitive observers are to sine-wave gratings of different spatial frequencies. The solid line through them is the MIRAGE prediction. The thin lines show the response gains of the individual filters and the S signals. Data points are from Campbell and Robson (1968).

threshold can be modified in one of two ways. If the second grating has a low contrast and a spatial frequency near the test, then the contrast threshold for the test will be reduced, the so-called *sub-threshold summation* (Sachs, Nachmias, & Robson, 1971). If the second grating has a high contrast and a spatial frequency near the first, then contrast threshold for the test will be elevated, the so-called *contrast masking* (Carter & Henning, 1971; Stromeyer & Julesz, 1972; Legge & Foley, 1980). An explanation for these effects will be described in the section "Analysis of S signals", p. 47; for the present it is enough to note that the spatial-frequency selectivity of the effect matches the selectivity of one R filter.

The final observation that suggests the presence of many filters of different sizes concerns the effects of observing a sine-wave grating pattern for a prolonged period of time. It is found that contrast threshold for that same grating or gratings of similar spatial frequency is raised as a consequence of some adaptation to the spatial frequency specific detection device (Blakemore & Campbell, 1969).

The conclusion is that more than one such process or filter must exist, because the frequency selectivity of the various effects are narrower than the selectivity of the whole system. Using techniques of these types, it has proved possible to construct quantitative models of the spatial filters (cf. Wilson, 1983, for example), although, because Wilson used a different assumption about how the output of the filters is used to detect the presence of contrast, a different range of filters is produced from those in this work.

Combination of Filter Outputs

Steps (2) and (3) concern how the outputs of the filters are combined in the visual system. The evidence for these two steps in the model is more direct than it is for the multiplicity of filters.

At first sight, one of the original observations that led to the idea of multiple independent filters would seem to be a counterexample to step (3) of MIRAGE. In MIRAGE, the filter outputs are combined before any decision about the presence of a stimulus is made on the basis of the size of the mass measurement. However, it has been found that sine-wave grating patterns of widely different spatial frequencies do not add together in their effect at contrast threshold (Campbell & Robson, 1968; Graham & Nachmias, 1971; Graham, Robson, & Nachmias, 1978). In the section "Analysis of S signals" I shall show that noise in the filter outputs leads to a very steep rise in mass for small increases in contrast around the threshold of the system. This means that any summation of different spatial frequencies would have a negligible effect on the threshold, even if the filter responses were summed together before deciding whether the stimulus was present.

There are circumstances where a high spatial frequency pattern can interfere with the detection of a low-frequency sine-wave grating. Henning, Hertz, and Broadbent (1975) measured the contrast threshold for detecting a low spatial frequency *target* grating in the presence of a high-frequency *carrier* grating with a *modulation* of contrast with the same period as the low-frequency target grating. Figure 2.10 shows the various stimuli involved in this experiment and the MIRAGE responses. Notice that the mask and the target are not entirely carried by separate filters, even though they are quite widely spaced in frequency.

The right-hand row of the figure shows the MIRAGE analysis of the stimuli from the Henning et al. (1975) study. Notice that as the target increases in amplitude, there is a sudden switch in the form of this analysis with the appearance of primitives of large mass and width, which correspond to those generated in response to the target on its own. These provide the cue to a subject trying to detect the target in the presence of the mask. Irrespective of the threshold for detecting the target on its own, the threshold contrast for detecting the target in the presence of the mask depends solely on the mask contrast. For the particular configuration illustrated, the target contrast needs to be the same as the mask contrast, which is exactly the finding of Henning et al. (1975).

Other configurations are possible. Nachmias and Rogovitz (1983) repeated this experiment for a range of masks in which the phase or position of the target was varied with respect to the position of the masking modulated carrier. Nachmias and Rogovitz (1983) found that the amount of threshold increase depended on the phase relationship between target and mask. The largest rise in threshold was found for the condition shown in Fig. 2.10. Consideration of the largest filter responses will show that MIRAGE provides a sufficient account for the data of Nachmias and Rogovitz (1983) as well as that of Henning et al. (1975).

These two experiments are important because they indicate that the mechanism that detects contrast signals in the output of the independent filters cannot access the filters independently. Another, and simpler demonstration of the same point is made by the experiments of Jamar and Koenderink (1985). These authors measured the contrast thresholds for

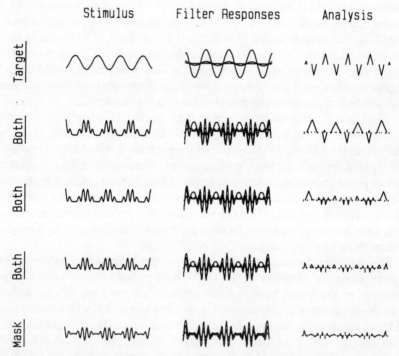

FIG. 2.10.   This figure illustrates some of the stimuli from the experiment by Henning et al. (1975) and the MIRAGE response to it. Notice that as the signal strength increases, the form of the analysis switches quite suddenly.

detecting randomly varying patterns of luminance, so-called noise stimuli, as a function of the *bandwidth* or range of spatial frequencies present in the random spatial fluctuations. They found no critical bandwidth phenomenon: The visual system always uses all the spatial luminance power in the target, irrespective of its bandwidth. This also matches the behaviour of MIRAGE.

There is other evidence for the combination of filter outputs that involves tasks other than contrast detection.

For example, Watt and Morgan (1983) found that when required to discriminate the degree of blur of an L-edge compared with a reference standard, subjects were less sensitive to an increment of blur added to a sharp edge than to one added to an edge blurred over about 5 arc min. This result is surprising for two reasons. First, it is rather counterintuitive. Second, it can be shown that the visual system is using the largest filters for this task, even though it would perform better for nearly sharp edges if it could access the smallest filters independently of the large ones. This point will be explained in detail in the next section. The conclusion is that small filters cannot be accessed independently of large filters.

The opposite of this is shown in a much reduced accuracy in localising a blurred edge (which is a large-scale task) accurately in the presence of irrelevant fine-scale structure (Watt & Morgan, 1984; Morgan & Watt, 1984). The quantitative details of these interactions could be accounted for by the specific proposal of the MIRAGE operation and some additional assumptions about the analysis of the S^+ and S^- signals, which can be supported by independent evidence (see the following). Watt and Morgan (1985) discuss other cases of interactions between different spatial scales or frequencies.

Analysis of S signals

We turn now to the evidence in support of the hypothesis that central moments of zero-bounded distributions are used to analyse the S^+ and S^- signals. This evidence is the most direct and simple to evaluate and it principally concerns the factors that determine how accurately the contrast, position, and blur of edges may be judged.

(1) *Contrast*: In a noise-free, ideal system there would be a directly proportional relationship between contrast in the stimulus and mass in the MIRAGE analysis. However, the human visual system is not noise-free, and as a result the relationship is distorted at low contrasts. The form of the relationship is shown in Fig. 2.11, which is based on an assumed Gaussian, white-noise process.

There are three departures from linearity (which is shown as a dotted line). At high contrasts there is some saturation that results in less than proportionate increases in mass. At very low contrasts, mass is almost constant,

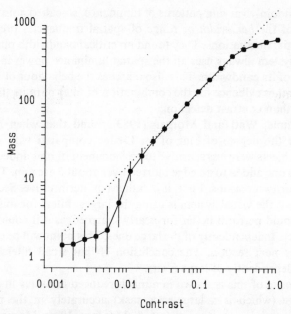

FIG. 2.11. The relationship between measured mass and physical stimulus contrast for a Gaussian blurred edge is plotted in this figure. The relationship is determined principally by the characteristics of intrinsic noise, and was obtained by Monte-Carlo simulations. Each data point represents the mean mass for 16 measures with different noise samples: The error bars are the standard deviations of the populations of estimates of mass.

irrespective of contrast. In this region the signal is effectively lost, and the mass that is measured is that due to noise alone. For slightly higher contrasts (about 0.01 on the figure), there is an accelerating non-linearity that corresponds approximately to $m = C^2$.

In this region the signal is beginning to be seen. The amplitude of the noise is still greater than that of the signal, and so any zero-bounded distribution corresponding to a part of the signal is split into several different masses. This can be seen in Fig. 2.12. This effect of the noise becomes less serious as contrast increases, hence the accelerating non-linearity gives way to a linearity. Figure 2.11 is very similar to the psychometric functions of Foley and Legge (1981, Fig. 2) and to the hypothetical transducer function of Nachmias and Sansbury (1974).

Figure 2.11 also shows, as vertical error bars, how the variability in the value of mass decreases with increasing contrast. This has implications for how accurately subjects can discriminate two different contrasts. Assume that a Weber's Law process applies to the comparison of two different masses. When subjects are asked to judge which of two stimuli has the greater contrast, then they must measure each mass and then compare the two

High Contrast

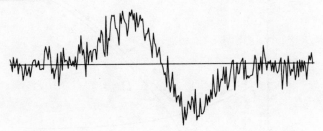

Medium Contrast

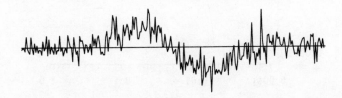

Low Contrast

FIG. 2.12.   Inspection of this figure shows that the visual system would often have a choice to make if it were to use zero-crossings or peaks as features that marked the location of luminance changes. If it knew precisely the form of the luminance change, then this choice could be made without much error. However it cannot, and so, particularly at low contrasts, errors would be inevitable.

measurements. Each step introduces its own independent error into the pattern of judgements, and the threshold contrast difference, dC, will represent the combination of a Weber's Law error, W_m, and a mass measurement error, E_m:

$$dC^2 = E_m{}^2 + W_m{}^2.$$

Figure 2.13 shows how these three terms vary with contrast. The data points are taken from a study by Legge and Kersten (1983) and match the theoretical predictions well.

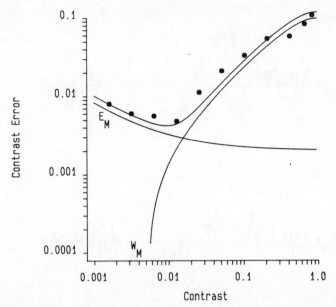

FIG. 2.13 .   The effects of errors in mass measurement, E_M, and comparison, W_M, on the discriminability of different degrees of contrast are drawn in this figure. The continuous lines are polynomial approximations to the Monte-Carlo simulations plotted in Fig. 2.11, and their vertical position is arbitrary with respect to the data points, which are taken from Legge and Kersten (1983). The MIRAGE fit to the data is close.

(2) *Position*: Contrast also has an effect on how accurately the position of an L-edge can be measured. As contrast is reduced, the ratio of signal amplitude to noise amplitude decreases. This results in a greater variability in where any particular feature in the response will be found. The predicted effects of contrast on spatial error for peaks, zero-crossings, and centroids are shown in Fig. 2.14, which is redrawn from Watt and Morgan (1985).

Reducing the edge contrast changes the signal to noise ratio in the S^+ and S^- signals, which in turn determines how accurately any candidate feature can be localised. Of the features considered, peaks, zero-crossings, and centroids, the centroids made the right prediction, and the other two did not. There is an interesting reason why this is the case, which illustrates an important axiom required to interpret the data properly.

Watt and Morgan started with the axiom that the visual system has no specific information about the stimulus. At low contrast this has a serious effect, as is illustrated in Fig. 2.12, which shows three different contrast levels. At the top, the highest contrast level, the noise has little influence on the positions of peak, zero-crossings, or centroid. At the bottom, for the lowest contrast level however, there are several distinct peaks and several zero-

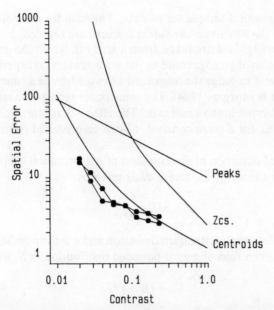

FIG. 2.14.   The random spatial error associated with judgements of edge location (dL) are plotted as a function of edge contrast. A value of 0.01 (1%) is used for the threshold of contrast detection. The functions for zero-crossings and centroids change slope at a contrast of about 0.1, that is, 1 log. unit above threshold. The two data functions are taken from a study reported by Watt and Morgan (1984), and the continuous functions are derived in the text. The vertical position of the data functions are arbitrary.

crossings to choose from. Because there are several zero-crossings, there are also several zero-bounded distributions each with a centroid, and so there are also several centroids to select from. What heuristic could the visual system use to make its choice? In the case of peaks, that at the greatest amplitude, i.e. the true maximum, would be the best choice. This predicts that location errors should increase in inverse proportion to the square root of contrast over the entire visible range of contrasts. In the case of zero-crossings, the most obvious heuristic would be to use the steepest. This predicts that location errors should rise in inverse proportion to contrast until contrast is about 1 log. unit above the visibility threshold, when the function should steepen, because the choice of which zero-crossing is then adding extra variability. In the case of centroids, that from the zero-bounded distribution with the largest mass would be a natural choice, and this predicts a square-root relationship down also to about 1 log. unit above contrast threshold and then a steeper rise in location errors, because of variability due to the selection heuristic. These three different predictions are shown in

Fig. 2.14 along with a sample set of data. The case for centroids is clearly supported and the other two candidate features are rejected.

The data on Fig. 2.14 are taken from a study in which the accuracy with which the location of an edge could be judged was assessed experimentally by requiring subjects to judge the alignment of two edges as a function of edge contrast (Watt & Morgan, 1984). The same paper reports the effects of edge blur on spatial error in the same task. The effects that blur, B, have on this spatial error, dL, for a given contrast, C, can be predicted from a statistical argument.

The standard deviation of the estimates of a distribution centroid (mean), i.e. the standard error of the mean, dL, is given by:

$$dL = \frac{k_1 s}{n^{\frac{1}{2}}}$$

where s is the distribution standard deviation and n is the number of samples (mass). For the centroid of a zero-bounded distribution in S, we have:

$$s = (B^2 + f^2)^{\frac{1}{2}}$$

by the convolution rule that variances add. For n, we require the integral of the zero-bounded response, i.e. the integral from minus infinity to zero (the location of the zero-crossing). The edge is expressed by:

$$\frac{C}{B(2\pi)^{\frac{1}{2}}} \int_{-\infty}^{x} \exp(-z^2/2B^2)\, dz$$

where C is contrast.
This is convolved with a filter with a filter:

$$(1 - x^2/f^2)\exp(-x^2/2f^2)$$

which gives as a response:

$$\frac{Cf^2}{(B^2+f^2)^{1\frac{1}{2}}} \exp(-x^2/2(B^2+f^2)).$$

Integrating between minus infinity and zero gives:

$$n = \frac{Cf^3}{(B^2+f^2)^{\frac{1}{2}}}$$

and therefore:

$$dL = \frac{K_1(B^2+f^2)^{\frac{1}{2}}(B^2+f^2)^{\frac{1}{2}}}{C^{\frac{1}{2}}f^{1\frac{1}{2}}}$$

for $B \gg f$ this becomes approximately:

$$dLaB^{1\frac{1}{2}}/C^{\frac{1}{4}}.$$

Figure 2.15 shows this function for a variety of values of f along with the data points. The function for f with a value of 2.83 arc min. fits the data well. This value is that expected for the MIRAGE algorithm, because the largest filter has the greatest effect on the spatial spread of the visual system.

(3) *Blur*: Watt and Morgan (1983) measured thresholds for discriminating the difference in the blur of two L-edges with various types and extents of blur. Subjects were presented with two edges and required to report which

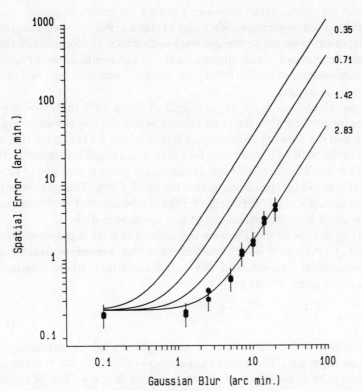

FIG. 2.15.   The predicted variations in spatial error (in locating edges) as a function of edge blur for four different sizes of filters. The data points are taken from Watt and Morgan (1984).

was the more blurred, so that for any given reference blurred edge, the sensitivity to extra blur could be measured. The finding was two-fold. First, for each of the different types of blurs, there was an optimum reference extent of blur, so that when the reference blur was less than or more than this optimum, sensitivity to an increment in blur was poorer. Second, for reference blur B larger than the optimum, the difference threshold dB was given by:

$$dB = k_b B^{1\frac{1}{2}}.$$

The exponent of $1\frac{1}{2}$ in this expression indicates that blur difference thresholds rise faster than they would be expected to according to Weber's Law, which is very unusual (see Laming, 1986).

Watt and Morgan (1983) went on to show that if blur was defined as the distance between the peak and trough in the second derivative of the stimulus, then the functions for a variety of different types of blurs followed exactly the same function. It was deduced that differential blur thresholds reflected two processes that in sequence localised the peak and trough and then measured their separation. Watt and Morgan (1984) showed that the unusual exponent was due to the accuracy with which the location of the peaks could be assessed. These arguments for peaks would apply to zero-bounded centroids, but would not apply to, say, zero-crossings and the slopes of zero-crossings.

A sample set of data is shown in Fig. 2.16 along with the theoretical predictions for various filter sizes and relative sensitivities as shown in Fig. 2.9. Notice that the data once again match a filter of size 2.83 arc min. This is equivalent to the MIRAGE operation for the case of a single isolated edge. It is clear that at low degrees of blur, the system could be more sensitive to blur than it is, if it could independently access the small filters. This has already been mentioned on p. 47 ff. as evidence for the combination of filter outputs. I shall now show how the predictions of this figure were derived.

We start by supposing that there are two sources of error in judgements of blur difference. One source is the measurement of blur, which is equivalent to the measurement of location, and this introduces errors, whose standard deviation, dL, is given by (see p. 52.):

$$dL = \frac{k_L (B^2 + f^2)^{\frac{3}{4}}}{C^{\frac{1}{2}} f^{1\frac{1}{2}}} \tag{1}$$

The other source is the comparison of measurements, which introduces a Weber's Law error dB_w. The actual measurement of blur B' that is made is determined by the convolution of the edge of blur B and a filter of space constant f:

$$B' = (B^2 + f^2)^{\frac{1}{2}} \tag{2}$$

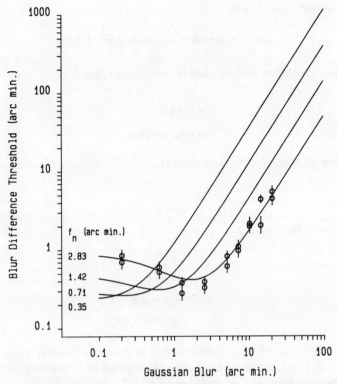

FIG. 2.16.   The predicted variation in blur difference threshold for four different sizes of filters. The data points are taken from Watt and Morgan (1983).

If we assume that the differential sensitivity to blur dB_w is the result of a Weber's law process on the comparison of internal blurs:

$$dB'_w = k_b B' \tag{3}$$

we then have:

$$B' + dB'_w = ((B + dB_w)^2 + f^2)^{\frac{1}{2}} \tag{4}$$

substituting (3), we have:

$$B'(1 + k_b) = ((B + dB_w)^2 + f^2)^{\frac{1}{2}}$$

substituting (2), we have:

$$(B^2 + f^2)^{\frac{1}{2}}(1 + k_b) = ((B + dB_w)^2 + f^2)^{\frac{1}{2}}$$

solving for dB_w, we obtain:

$$dB_w = -B + (B^2 + (k_b^2 + 2k_b)(B^2 + f^2))^{\frac{1}{2}} \qquad (5)$$

It can now be shown that dB_w has its minimum value for:

$$B = f/(l + k_b)$$
$$= f \text{ for small } k_b.$$

We can go a step further and show that if we consider a sharp edge, given by:

$$B = 0$$

we then have that:

$$B' = f$$
$$dB'_w = k_b f$$
$$f(1 + k_b) = (dB_w^2 + f^2)^{\frac{1}{2}}$$

and
$$dB_w = f(k_b^2 + 2k_b)^{\frac{1}{2}}.$$

This shows that dB_w is proportional to f in the case of a sharp edge, and so the smallest blur sensitivity in this case is obtained by examining the output of the smallest filter, as one would expect.

Finally, the complete predictions for blur difference discrimination, dB, are obtained by combining the effects of dL (equation 1) and dB_w (equation 5):

$$dB = (dL^2 + dB_w^2)^{\frac{1}{2}}.$$

These are the predictions shown in Fig. 2.16.

The Interpretation of the Primitive Measurements

The final type of evidence concerns the phenomenology of how waveforms appear to the observer. If we assume that an L-edge, an L-line, and a luminance plateau are all perceived veridically, then we are led to the three interpretive rules. There are two cases where these rules fail however, and these are shown in Fig. 2.17. On the left is a luminance ramp edge, which is a stimulus that gives rise to Mach bands, and on the right is the stepping luminance waveform, which gives rise to the Chevreul illusion (cf. Cornsweet, 1970, p. 276). In the left-hand case, provided that the ramp is longer

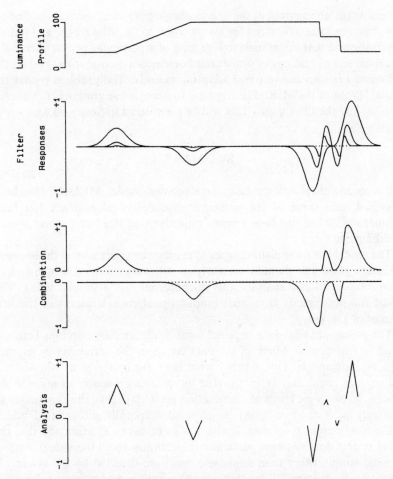

FIG. 2.17.   The top of this figure shows a luminance profile with two features in it that the
MIRAGE interpretation scheme incorrectly represents. On the left is a linear luminance
gradient, which causes Mach bands. It can be seen in the bottom row that the centre of the
gradient is misinterpreted as a region where luminance does not change. On the right is the
double step stimulus that causes the Chevreul illusion. In this case the centre where luminance is
not changing is not resolved by the largest filter.

than about 5 arc min., the filters all resolve a region of zero-response in the
centre of the ramp, because being second derivative filters, they are insensitive to luminance gradients. In the right-hand case, the filters all fail to
resolve a region of zero-response in the middle of the step, because the edges
are spread out too far. This means that in each case, the line rule is used to
interpret the response distributions, rather than the edge rule, and as a
consequence Mach band type phenomena are seen in each case.

It is worth noting that, at the phenomenological level, there is one finding that seems to raise difficulties for this account so far. Blakemore and Sutton (1969) showed that adaptation to a grating of a particular period altered the perceived size of gratings of similar but not identical period to exaggerate the difference between the test and adapting periods. The problem is that the spatial layout of the MIRAGE response to a sine-wave grating is not altered by adjusting the filter gains. This will be considered in Section 3.4.

SUMMARY

In this second chapter of the essay, an algorithm/model, MIRAGE, has been described, and some of the pertinent psychophysical evidence has been summarised. It has not been a prime objective that this latter aspect should be exhaustive.

The model has three distinct types of process: an operation on the image in the image plane and domain, an analysis of the transformed image, and an interpretation of the analysis into phenomenal and symbolic terms. The model follows directly from the computational considerations of the first chapter of this essay.

The psychophysical data required some additional assumptions before it could be interpreted. Much of the data concerns the variability of psychophysical judgements: This is really what is meant by the term "threshold", and so data could only be interpreted by assuming a source of noise in the process. In photopic levels of illumination (as in daylight), this is assumed to be largely intrinsic white noise (spatially and temporally uncorrelated) added to the filter output responses. It also has to be taken as axiomatic that the visual system does not have particular information about individual psychophysical stimuli other than as those stimuli are detected by the system: It cannot set up matched filters that are optimum for a particular task.

THE SECOND PROBLEM

The psychophysical data relied largely on inadequacies, distortions, and errors in the behaviour of MIRAGE. How are these apparent shortcomings avoided in perception? This is the subject matter of the third chapter of this essay.

3
Measurements, Metrics, and Distortions

In the preceding two chapters a specification of the goals of the Primal Sketch has been described, with some indication of the general types of operations that are required to accomplish those goals, followed by an account of a model for part of the Primal Sketch as it exists in human vision. Essentially, the MIRAGE model takes an image and replaces it with two new S images. These are then parsed into their zero-bounded response distributions that are each characterised by their mass, centroid, and perhaps standard deviation.

Take the case of luminance edges. These give rise to one response distribution in each of the two S signals. The centroid of each is measured, and the value of the blur of the L-edge and its position are then calculated from these two centroids. But at this point we must be careful to avoid being misled into supposing that assigning values to blur and position is straightforward.

Why is it not straightforward? Take the case of blur first. The blurs are all changed by MIRAGE. We are tempted to suppose that this has to be corrected, but of course this is to misunderstand the process of measurement. A "sharp" edge is just the least blurred that is experienced. There is no more need to correct it so that its blur is zero than there is need to turn the inverted image in the eye back up the right way.

The case of position is a little more complicated. It is usual to define an edge as a sudden change in luminance, i.e. luminance discontinuity (e.g. Canny, 1984; Spacek, 1985). In order to find such features, the current practice is to use linear filters that are optimised both to preserve the correct location of the feature with as high accuracy as possible, and to have a high sensitivity for detecting low-contrast edges. The need for high sensitivity is obvious and easy to understand. The fact that filter design incorporates constraints that require the accurate localisation of the edge to be optimal needs some explanation. If we take the luminance discontinuity definition of an edge, then the actual L-edges and lines that appear in images can be described as being the joint effect of a luminance discontinuity at one specific place in the image and a blurring function, which will also be specific to each instance. The correct location of the edge can be defined as the location of the unblurred underlying discontinuity. The difficulty is that this correct location often cannot be found because the filters respond to nearby contours as well, and their outputs are accordingly distorted in a variety of different ways.

MEASURING IMAGE ATTRIBUTES

As we have seen in Chapter 2, a luminance edge gives rise to two adjacent distributions of response, one in each of the S signals. Each distribution is dispersed over an area of the S signal space, but can be assigned a location in that space by its centroid. The physical distance between the two centroids, B', is related to the blur of the edge, B, by the expression:

$$B' = (B^2 + f^2)^{\frac{1}{2}}$$

where f is the space constant of the filter. The shape of this function is drawn in Figure 3.1. Blur is distorted by the system. The function is reversible, so that given B' and f, the blur of the edge, B, can be calculated:

$$B = (B'^2 - f^2)^{\frac{1}{2}}$$

In this way the distortion of the edge blur by the filters can be corrected and the blur of a sharp edge will be registered as zero.

A Metric for Blur

When we measure a distance v, we take a unit magnitude distance u, and count how many, n, we need to fill the distance. In other words: $v = nu$. In so doing we have arbitrarily defined a *scale* by selecting a particular unit, and defined an *origin*, which is the value of n for distances that are less than u. In this case the origin is zero. The scale and origin are necessary devices, but their specification is arbitrary. The scale is defined to be linear in this example, because the magnitude of u is fixed. If u increased by a fixed factor

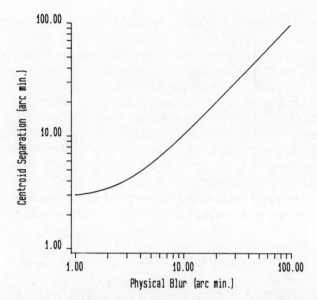

FIG. 3.1. The function relating centroid separation (which ranges from 3' upwards) to physical blur (which ranges from 0' upwards).

each time it was used to fill a particular distance, then the scale would be logarithmic. The way in which a scale changes is the *scale function*.

The three properties of origin, scale, and the scale function define a *metric*. In practice, the values for each are chosen by their convenience and reliability. What choices would be most appropriate in a sensory system? Let us start with an assertion: "The metric is chosen so that any particular measurement is equally as likely as any other." This assertion has some interesting consequences that I shall now explore.

Figure 3.2 shows a plausible distribution of physical edge blurs. Figure 3.3 shows the same distribution of blurs, but now as seen through the MIRAGE operation (the exact distribution is not known). Notice that the smallest blur has a size that is well above zero. The physical measure of blur is according to a scale that you and I have adopted, by agreement, in order to be able to discuss blur. The scale for MIRAGE blur is the same as that for physical blur and so there is not a linear relationship. Marked by thin vertical lines are the boundaries between scale units that would have the property of each being used on 10% of occasions. Notice that they are not equal in physical size; the area under the frequency distribution that is bounded by two such lines is, however, constant. The size of any scale unit is determined by the frequency of blurs at that point on the scale. Figure 3.4 shows how this new scale relates

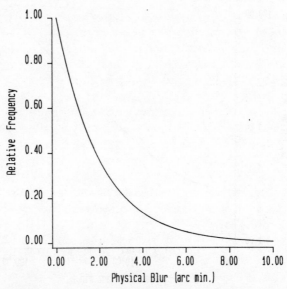

FIG. 3.2.   A plausible distribution of the frequencies of physical blurs in images. Note that the distribution is one-sided.

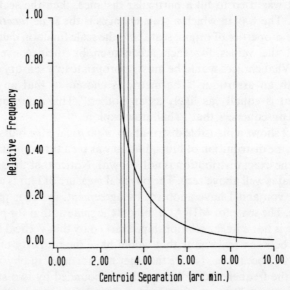

FIG. 3.3.   The equivalent distribution for the distribution of MIRAGE centroid separations. The thin vertical lines would be the boundaries between units on an ordinal scale.

62

to the physical scale. Notice that the relationship is not linear: This is because the distribution of physical edge blur measurements is not uniform.

Although this discussion is offered in the terms of large, discrete units, there is no implication that the perception or sensation of magnitudes is quantised. The units could support an interpolation process, just as do the scale markings on a metre rule.

The next question to be tackled is how such a metric might be constructed. The system could do what I did to create the example: Place its scale unit boundaries at points where the area under the distribution frequency curve on the physical metric was equalised. However, if it had the physical metric given, most of the need for metric would be satisfied, and there would be little point in going through with the exercise. In fact, all that is necessary is that the system has a store of blurs that it has experienced that are sorted into an approximate order of magnitude.

An analogy helps. Imagine that each experience is presented by a bead with a particular mass that represents the blur magnitude. The beads are then simply arranged in one long row so that their masses are in order: Each bead is placed so that all those on one side are lighter than it and all those on the other side are heavier. This line of bead now actually defines the metric. The "heaviness" of any bead is represented by the number of places along the line to the point where it would be placed. There is one very powerful property of

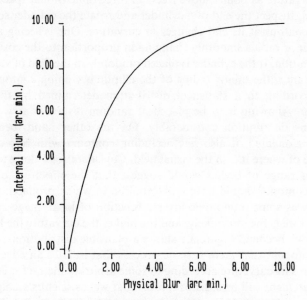

FIG. 3.4.   The relationship between physical blur and its internal measure.

such a system. It is *error-correcting*. Suppose that every bead is subject to a systematic error that is a monotonic function of its mass, such as squaring or a log. transform. These do not affect the ordering of the beads and so the mapping from physical metric to internal metric is unaffected.

Returning to the case of edge blur, it follows from this argument that the monotonic transformation that maps from blur into centroid separations does not matter. There is no need to correct it! See Fig. 3.4.

A Metric for Curvature

The blur distribution is one-sided: All blurs are greater than some minimum in any monotonic metric. How about an L-edge attribute that does not have this property? An example is curvature that ranges from minus infinity, through zero, to plus infinity. What is the appropriate metric to choose for curvature? The distribution of contour curvatures from natural scenes is fixed by constraints. We can note several constraints on the curvature of surface occlusions and the image contours projected by them. The mean curvature is bound to be zero: A body that projects an occluding contour with curvature in a particular direction can be turned around freely so that the sign of the curvature changes. Bodies are generally distributed across the field of view in a haphazard fashion and so, on average, the mean (signed) contour curvature will be zero. The distribution of curvatures about zero is probably also fairly stable across scenes, because the transformations of contour curvature as bodies move freely in three-dimensional space are also constrained. Inspect the end of a cylinder and rotate the cylinder so that the occluding contour at its end changes in curvature. One is seeing an ellipse with the minor radius smoothly changing in proportion to the cosine of the angle of rotation. If the cylinder is placed randomly in the field of view but at a fixed distance, the minor radius of the elliptic occluding contour will be imaged according to a statistical distribution determined by this cosine relationship. Allowing it to be placed at random distances as well would disperse this distribution considerably. On the other hand, because the cylinder is elongated, it also has occluding contours with zero-curvature irrespective of where it is in the visual field. Considerations along these lines for a wider range of bodies would suggest that the curvature of imaged occluding contours should have a distribution in which probability density would vary as some monotonic inverse function of local image curvature. Zero-curvature is the most likely, and the higher the curvature the less likely such contours become. Figure 3.5 shows a plausible distribution.

Let us suppose that there is some process that isolates an edge segment and measures its curvature according to some arbitrary metric for curvature. This measurement will be a distortion of what we, as scientists, might think of as the true curvature. For example, because of an "error" in geometric

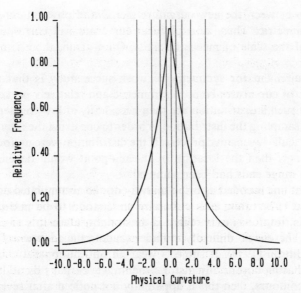

FIG. 3.5. The possible distribution of edge curvatures in images, on the physical scale of (radius) −1. The thin vertical lines show how an ordinal scale might appear. Note that symmetry is preserved.

optics, straight occluding edges project curved L-edges when they are imaged onto peripheral, off-axis parts of the retina. It is only our expectations of the behaviour of flat images, such as photographs, that makes this strange. The retina is properly described as a hemispherical (nearly) surface or manifold. This has consequences for the image: It turns it upside-down and curves straight lines compared with our naive expectations.

Andrews (1964) considered the application of error-correcting codes for the transmission of contour curvatures. The general idea was that if the frequency distribution of curvatures in the input to the visual system is stable and known, then it is possible to examine the frequency distribution of curvature measurements as output and make the necessary adjustments to align the two.

I take this idea a little further. The value of zero physical curvature has an important status. Symmetry relates physical curvatures that are the same distance from zero but on opposite sides. Suppose that we just take an ordering of measured curvatures from minus infinity to plus infinity. Remember that this is all we can do: We do not know where zero-curvature is yet. Once this is done, we can assume that any bias error in curvature has been automatically taken out, just as it had for blur in the previous example. If the distribution of physical curvatures is symmetric, then it follows that the relationship between the new curvature metric and physical curvature will also be symmetric. Thus, zero physical curvature will correspond to the midpoint of the scale of measured units. Once again, there is no need to correct!

The requirement for symmetry to work successfully is that the actual distribution of curvatures be both symmetric and relatively peaked at zero. The tails of such a distribution are then necessarily at low frequencies. This means that sampling the distribution in order to construct the internal metric is not a particularly sensitive process. If the distribution were uniform over its effective range, then the location of the midpoint would depend on how reliably the range ends had been sampled.

A straight line is coded as being midway on the accumulated distribution of measured curvatures, and is thereby understood to be midway on the expected distribution, i.e. is regarded as straight. Once this argument has been made, there is no difficulty in understanding the adaptation and after-effects of Gibson (1933). If subjects wear an optical apparatus in front of their eyes that monotonically distorts the image, perhaps by adding curvature to all contours, then this is apparently not noticed after several weeks, but once vision is restored to natural optics, the opposite distortion is experienced and takes some time to fade away. The time course of such phenomena might be the interval over which the measured density distribution is assessed.

Other Image Attributes

Are there other types of spatial measurements that have predictable underlying image probabilities? Note that the important point is that the probability distributions are constrained. There has been little attempt to measure the statistics of natural scenes, but there are several studies that make important contributions. Srinivasan, Laughlin, and Dubs (1982) looked at a small number of scenes and measured spatial autocorrelation functions. These assess the degree of correlation of the grey-level values at any two different points on the image as a function of their separation: They reflect the spatial frequency spectrum of the image. Burton and Moorhead (in press) have measured the typical spatial frequency spectrum directly for natural images and find that it tends to lie close to a function in which amplitude is inversely proportional to spatial frequency. These studies do not directly prove that L-edge and L-line separations have predictable image distributions, but they are suggestive. It is therefore not surprising to learn that prolonged inspection of a scene where one particular spatial separation predominates causes altered perception of space and spatial intervals (Blakemore & Sutton, 1969). Specifically, adaptation to a high-contrast grating pattern alters the subsequent perceived size of the bars of gratings within about one octave of the adaptation frequency. A grating of the same frequency is not perceptibly different after adaptation compared with before, but a slightly lower frequency grating is seen as being rather lower in frequency than it actually is, and symmetrically a grating higher in frequency than the adapting stimulus is perceived as even higher still. These findings are illustrated graphically in Fig. 3.6. The reader will be able to construct the explanation for this phenomenon without difficulty.

Another dimension for which there is a predictable distribution is contrast in natural images (MacKerras, Bossomaier, & Laughlin, in press). Most contrasts are less than 30%, irrespective of illumination conditions, but a small proportion of contrasts are much higher. Notice that we now have two

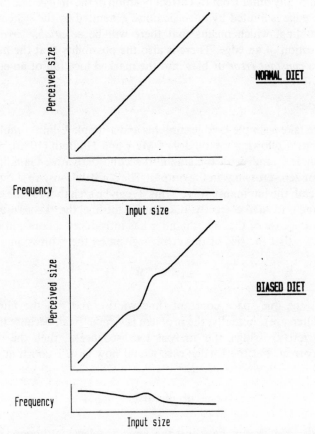

FIG. 3.6. The effect of introducing an abnormal distribution of input sizes to a self-calibrating measurement system. At the top, a normal diet leads to a linear relationship between input size and calibrated response (perceived size). At the bottom, one input size predominates, and a non-linear effect is obtained.

reasons for using luminance differences. The first came from the definition of scene features and how they are imaged; the second comes from how the intensity-based measurements can be understood.

DISTORTIONS IN EDGE LOCATION

I shall use the term *location* to refer to the point in an image where a particular indication of a luminance edge or line exists. The term *position* refers to that point in the image that corresponds to the visual direction in which lies the physical cause of the L-edge.

There are two different ways in which the marked location of an edge in the edge map may differ from its correct position in the image. The process of finding the edge is limited by intrinsic noise generated by the system and by spatial sampling, which means that there will be a *variable error* in the marked location of an edge. There is also the possibility that the filters will introduce a *constant error* or bias into the marked location of an edge.

Single Edges

Suppose we take a simple L-edge stimulus and a simple L-line stimulus, as in Fig. 3.7 (top). Following the theory of Marr and Hildreth (1980), we could convolve these stimuli with the standard second derivative Gaussian filter, and look for zero-crossings in the output. The convolutions are shown in the figure, beneath the luminance waveforms. It can be seen that for the edge, the zero-crossing is located correctly, but that for the line, the two zero-crossings are not. In the case of the line, the filter has introduced a constant error. It can be shown that the size of this error is given by the expression:

$$\pm (B^2 + f^2)^{\frac{1}{2}}$$

where B is the line space constant (line width), and f is the filter space constant (filter size). Actually, the problem is symmetrical, because if instead of seeking zero-crossings, the analysis localised peaks, then the line case would be correct, but the L-edge case would now have a constant error of size:

$$\pm (B^2 + f^2)^{\frac{1}{2}}.$$

Centroids, *à la mirage*, have just the same problems, although there is a rather simple solution, which is to take the *centroid-of-centroids*; because symmetry is presented by the filters, the centroid-of-centroids is aligned with the L-edge and also with the L-line.

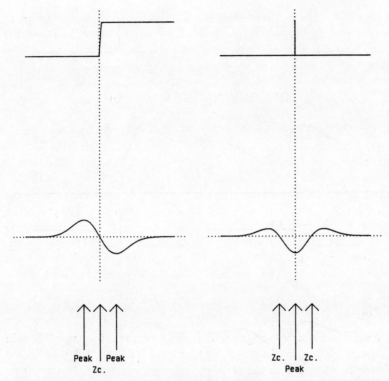

FIG. 3.7. At the top are shown the luminance profiles for an idealised step edge, and an idealised line. Aligned beneath these are their smoothed second derivatives. Notice that the zero-crossing is aligned with the edge but not with the line, and the peak is aligned with the line but not the edge.

In human vision, variable errors are generally very small but constant errors may be very much larger (Moulden & Renshaw, 1979), at least for blurred edges (Mather & Morgan, 1986). This is easily understood in terms of a compressive non-linearity, which preserves the symmetry for a sharp edge but not for blurred edges. Mather and Morgan showed that the zero-crossings following an intensity non-linearity could match the constant errors. The centroid-of-centroids will follow the zero-crossing closely.

Two Adjacent Edges

There is another form of distortion to be found in the output of linear filters of any particular spatial scale. When two edges or lines lie closer together than the size of the filter, it is not possible to decide reliably from the filter output whether there are two features or one: They cannot be resolved. This

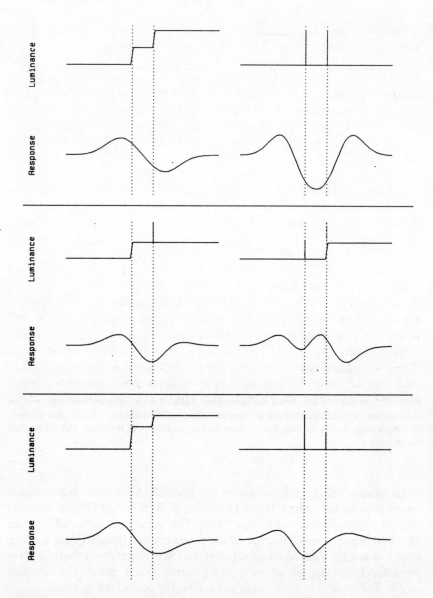

FIG. 3.8. At the top are shown the luminance profiles for a double step edge, and a double line. Aligned beneath these are their smoothed second derivatives. Beneath these are shown the luminance profiles for two composite step edge plus line stimuli. Aligned beneath these are their smoothed second derivatives. At the bottom are shown the luminance profiles for an unequal double step edge, and an unequal double line. Aligned beneath these are their smoothed second derivatives. Notice that neither zero-crossings nor peaks are now aligned with any of the edges or the lines.

70

is illustrated in Fig. 3.8 for the simplest case where the two features are identical (at the top), and for the case of a mixture of a line and an edge (middle). In both these cases, the zero-crossings, peaks, and centroids all reflect a sort of average location for the image features, as does the case at the bottom when the two features have different amplitudes. In none of these cases, do zero-crossings, peaks, or whatever, correspond to the location of one or other image feature: There is always a constant error with respect to the individual lines and edges, which is determined by both the filter size and the stimulus layout. Figure 3.9 shows the locations of zero-crossings in the response of a filter to two parallel edges as a function of edge separation. The dotted lines mark the correct location of the edge, and the solid lines show the location of zero-crossings. The filter has a space constant of 2.8 arc min. If the edges are five times this distance apart, then the zero-crossings are in the correct location. If the edges are between three and five times this distance, the zero-crossings are still in the correct location, but there is now an extra one at the centre. If the edges are two to three times the filter space constant apart, then there is significant distortion in the zero-crossing location, and for the smallest separations resolution fails. This pattern applies only to two sharp edges of equal contrast. Any other arrangement would lead to a different pattern of distortion.

When we turn to the MIRAGE behaviour in respect of a double step edge, shown in Fig. 3.10, we can see that it preserves more of the information in an undistorted fashion. Nevertheless, the problem still exists. One way in which to avoid this problem might be to use a special heuristic rule to correct for

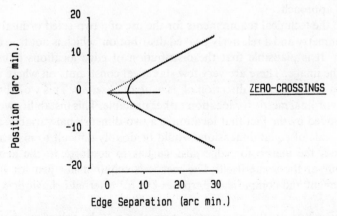

FIG. 3.9.   The location of the zero-crossings in the output of a filter in response to a double step edge (as in Fig. 3.8) are drawn as a function of the separation of the edges. The dotted lines are the actual edge locations.

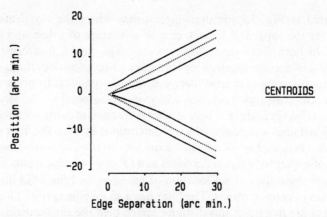

FIG. 3.10.   The positions of the zero-bounded centroids for a double step edge are drawn as a function of the separation between the edges. The dotted lines are the actual edge position. Notice how the centroids preserve more detail at small separation than the zero-crossings did in Fig. 3.9.

such a problem. Marr and Hildreth (1980) proposed something similar. This is not a very practical solution because of the free way in which edges may approach each other.

The Problems with Edge Distortion

Distortions in L-edge location occur, so why not use error-correcting code metrics to compensate? There are two fundamental problems that prevent such an approach.

First, the technical requirements for the use of a two-sided ordinal metric were symmetry and a relatively peaked distribution, which is not true of edge location. It is plausible that the distribution of edge locations is uniform across the image. There are very few statistical constraints on where a body can be in relation to the direction of gaze of an observer. This would tend to make an ordinal metric for location rather unstable. This instability would be compounded by the fact that location is a two-dimensional variable, and an ordinal scale of equal dimensions would be doubly difficult to maintain.

Second, the metric for edge *position* has to conform to the geometric behaviour of the scene itself. The metric is required not just for internal measurement and comparison purposes but for external behaviour within a fixed space.

I shall return to the question of how this may be solved in the fourth chapter of the essay, but before that I describe a striking phenomenon that makes the difficulties of edge locations and positions even more interesting.

THE "PHENOMENAL PHENOMENON" AND MIRAGE

The "phenomenal phenomenon" is a name devised by Gregory and Heard (1983) to describe the unexpected effects they observed in a simple display comprising only four luminances. The display has a long central grey region; at one end there is a thin brighter stripe; at the other end there is a thin darker stripe; beyond these there is a background luminance that is the same on both sides. Gregory and Heard made three interesting discoveries: first, the perceived position of each stripe depends on the value of the background luminance; second, the two narrow stripes move from side to side when the background luminance is modulated up and down over a 0.2 log. unit range of luminance; third, the way in which the seen position of the stripes varies with background has the opposite sign to the seen movement of the stripes!

The Static Phenomenon

The phenomenal phenomenon is a particularly striking example of the distortions associated with filters. The stimuli involved are essentially one-dimensional, and their luminance waveforms are drawn on the left of Fig. 3.11. The central region is a mid-grey-level of luminance; at one end there is a narrow dark bar, and at the other, a light bar; beyond these the waveform is set to one of seven values ranging from darker than the dark bar to lighter than the bright bar. The static phenomenon is that the apparent position of the light and dark bars depends on the luminance of the end regions (data points on Fig. 3.13). These findings may be accounted for by the MIRAGE algorithm. The S^+ and S^- signals for the same sample conditions of background luminance are also shown in Fig. 3.11.

Figure 3.12 shows where the various individual centroids are as a function of background luminance. It also shows where the centroid-of-centroids is for the light stripe and for the dark stripe. Figure 3.13 shows the offset between these two and also the data measured by Gregory and Heard (1983). The agreement is close.

The Moving Phenomenon

The moving phenomenon is that when the background luminance is modulated through a 0.2 log. unit range the thin stripes appear to move in counterphase.

Take the thin lines of Fig. 3.12, that is, the individual centroid positions, and calculate in which direction each centroid moves, and by how much, as luminance is increased. These are shown in Fig. 3.14. We now have a new series of estimates of how the stimulus might apparently be moving when the background luminance is changed. These are different for each centroid, just

Luminance profile $S^+ : S^-$

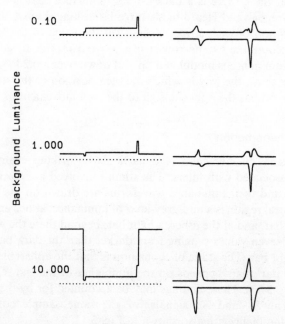

FIG. 3.11.   This figure shows on the left the luminance profiles for some of the stimuli of the Gregory and Heard (1983) study, and on the right, the S signals that result.

as the position error measurements were, and so the visual system might take an average value. This average moving displacement error is plotted as a continuous heavy line in Fig. 3.14. The effective movement between the two stripes is shown in Fig. 3.15 along with the data points. The resemblance is less convincing, but still fairly close. A proper motion-detection model would undoubtedly come closer.

The Border-locking Phenomenon

The phenomenal phenomenon has highlighted a serious computational problem, which is aptly described by the term "border locking" introduced by Gregory and Heard (1979). Recall that I made a distinction between the

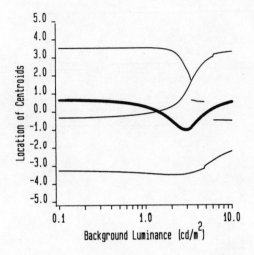

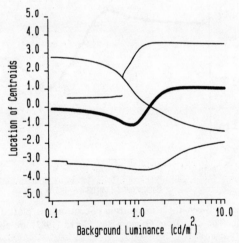

FIG. 3.12. The constant spatial error associated with the positions of the various zero-bounded centroids in the static MIRAGE response to the stimuli of Gregory and Heard (1983) are drawn as dotted lines. At the top are the responses around the light stripe; below are those around the dark stripe. In each case the heavy line is the centroid-of-centroids.

derived *location* of an L-edge feature in the image and the derived *position* or visual direction of the physical cause of the edge feature. The reason for this distinction is now easy to explain. Location is one source of information concerning position, but there are potentially others.

The phenomenal phenomenon has shown that different cues to position can be in conflict. During the moving phenomenon, where is the thin stripe of

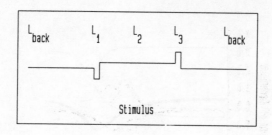

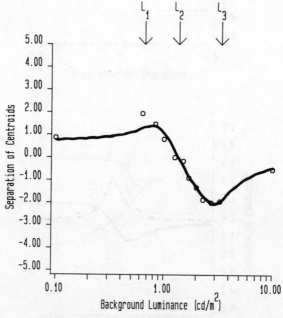

FIG. 3.13.   The offset between the two centroid-of-centroids is plotted as a function of background luminance. The data from Gregory and Heard (1983) are also shown, and the agreement is close.

luminance at any one instant? It could be at the centroid-of-centroids, but that would be to require that it moved in the opposite direction to that in which it is perceived to have moved. Or vice versa. There is clearly a problem here that I shall discuss in the next chapter.

SUMMARY

The MIRAGE operation was described in Chapter 2 as a sequence of operations on the image. The effect of these operations is to produce a

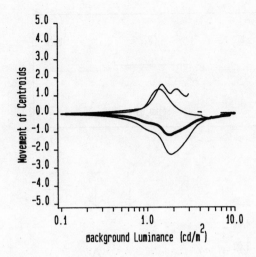

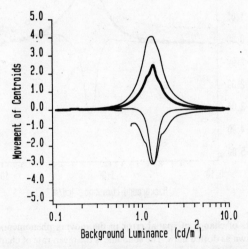

FIG. 3.14. Movements of the various centroids for a 0.2 log. unit rise in luminance are shown. These plots are basically just the derivatives of Fig. 3.12. The heavy lines show the average.

representation in terms of the location of centroids of zero-bounded response distributions. In this section, I have begun to consider how the output of MIRAGE can be interpreted.

An easy example of the difficulties that are encountered was the case of measuring the blur of an edge. An L-edge produces two centroids whose separation is a non-linear transformation of the blur of the edge. It is tempting to suggest a deblurring type of compensation, but I have argued

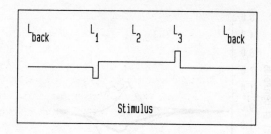

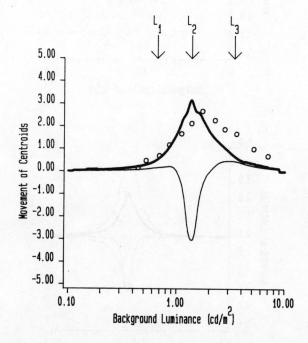

FIG. 3.15. The rate of change of spatial error in the moving phenomenon of Gregory and Heard (1983) are drawn as dotted lines. The solid line is the mean rate of change of spatial error of all centroids, each weighted by its own mass. Note that this is not the same as the rate of change of the mean spatial position error (thin line), and actually has the opposite sign.

that an ordinal metric (in essence) based on frequency of occurrence removes this need.

A second example came from a consideration of how the curvature of an edge might be measured. Unlike blur, this is not bounded at zero (despite our conceptions of the singularity of zero-curvature), but it is, however, likely to be symmetrically distributed, which once again allows an ordinal metric to be used.

These metrics are very generally error correcting, being essentially blind to any monotonic distortions of the attributes that are being measured.

I then turned to the question of distortions in the locations of L-edge features in the image because of neighbouring contours. These distortions in the edge blur could be corrected, in principle, by analytic heuristics. There are some obstacles that prevent the use of error-correcting ordinal metrics for location. Location is a two-dimensional attribute; and it is uniformly distributed within its bounds.

This chapter concluded with a description of a striking "phenomenal phenomenon" that shows a dissociation between, on the one hand, the location of an L-edge and how this can change, and on the other hand, the motion of the edge.

THE THIRD PROBLEM

The location of an L-edge and its motion are both cues to the position of the physical cause of the luminance change. There are many others in addition. These need not agree. What is to be done?

4 Calculating Values for Spatial Position with Grouping

In the previous chapters, I started by examining how luminance in images was related to surface creases and discontinuities. It was found necessary to take a second derivative of the luminance to find all the interesting image features. It was also found necessary to take the second derivative over a range of different spatial scales, so that surface texture did not obscure real edges. This left a practical difficulty of how to combine into a single representation information from the various spatial scales. MIRAGE was offered as an algorithm that achieved this in an interesting fashion, because it seemed to preserve both fine detail and long-range structure, but separately. It was shown to group small neighbouring details, but no compelling computational advantage for this has yet been offered.

In the third chapter, the significance of spatial measurements on the output of the MIRAGE transformation was examined. The answer is complicated because linear filters inevitably create distortions. Some distortions are not important because they can be corrected by properties of ordinal scales. This is possible for attributes such as curvature and blur that have predictable distributions of values in natural images that are related monotonically to reliable but distorted distributions of values in the cumulative populations of measurements made.

The two image quantities for which this rule does not apply are spatial location and luminance. It is therefore necessary to take the derivatives of these qualities, separation and contrast, which do have predictable statistics. However, a representation with only these attributes is not complete. It does not, for example, make explicit the relative luminance of two unconnected parts of the image. Contrast is explicit only between adjacent patches of the image, i.e. where luminance changes, and so there is no explicit comparison of luminance across more than one contour in this representation. Some calculation and representation of absolute grey-level for each part of the image seems necessary.

The representation of feature separations has the same drawbacks. The separation between one image contour and any other is not explicitly represented because it is only the separation between one image contour and its immediate neighbours that is drawn from a statistically stable distribution. Any visual task that requires information about separations across several contours must use a representation in which L-edge locations are explicit or all possible pairwise contour separations are explicit.

This full representation will contain two types of measurement: those that are strictly *local*, such as orientation, length, curvature, blur; and those that are *global* relative to the structure of the image, such as location and brightness. What is the distinction?

Consider the difference between line curvature and line location. In order to compute the curvature of a line, the only information about itself that the system requires is the topological relationship of one pixel to its neighbours (for those pixels that are active) and a stored distribution of past experience. In order to compute contour location, the system needs the equivalent information for spatial separations plus a spatial co-ordinate system with origin and axes because these cannot be derived from image statistics. This metric for position is an arbitrary adjunct, and as a result, the significance of any position measurement is with respect only to the global structure of the image.

ERRORS THAT PROPAGATE THROUGH AN ABSOLUTE REPRESENTATION

Consider how luminance might be reconstructed from a series of luminance difference measurements. This is an easy case to visualise, and we shall start with a one-dimensional analysis. Figure 4.1 shows a one-dimensional slice through a pattern with a variety of blurred luminance step edges across it. Immediately below the stimulus waveform is an ideal representation of the pattern created without error or distortion. Each edge is marked at its measured position by a chevron, the height of which is a code for the luminance difference and the width of which is a code for the degree of blur. The original signal can be reconstructed by dividing each chevron by its width (so that its area is now a code for the luminance change across the edge) and then integrating. The result of this is shown in the third row. The

Exact Analysis

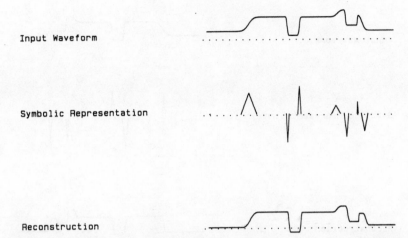

Input Waveform

Symbolic Representation

Reconstruction

FIG. 4.1. The top line shows a luminance profile, which contains seven edges with different positions, blurs, and contrasts. Beneath this is shown an analysis of the edges in the luminance profile, each edge, which is marked by a chevron placed at the edge position, has a width equal to the blur of the edge, and an amplitude equal to the edge contrast. The final row shows a reconstruction of the waveform.

integration is simply an algebraic convenience for reconstruction of the signal: Integration computes areas in the chevron and allows the accumulation of the effects across the result. It is not suggested as a visual process.

Now suppose we introduce a random error into the measure of blur at each of the edges, and then attempt to reconstruct the signal from each end: Once again the result does not depend on which end the integration begins from, as seen in Fig. 4.2, although this time the reconstruction has blur errors. Nevertheless, all the edges are at the correct positions, and the various luminance plateaus are all at the correct levels. The effects of the blur error are not spread across the image. This can be described by stating that blur is a *local measure* and a *local attribute*: Any errors in its estimation cause strictly local distortions in the representation.

This is not the case for errors in the luminance difference (contrast) measurements, as can be seen from Fig. 4.3. The luminance input waveform is at the same intensity level at each end. The reader should think of it as being a circular slice through an image, so that the ends are really to be joined to each other. When there is an error in one of the luminance difference measurements, the calculated luminance at the two ends, which should be the same, are not: They differ by the amount of the error. If each luminance difference measurement had an error, the difference between the two estimates of the end luminance is the sum of all the errors. Exactly the same

Blur Errors

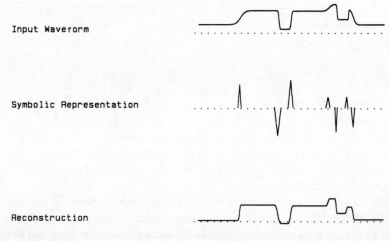

Input Waverorm

Symbolic Representation

Reconstruction

FIG. 4.2.   This is the same as Fig. 4.1, except that there are errors in the analysis of the edge blurs. Notice that the effects of these errors are restricted in the reconstruction to the locus of the edges in each image.

Contrast Errors

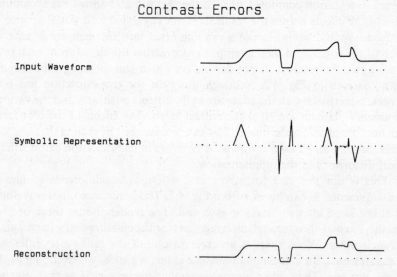

Input Waveform

Symbolic Representation

Reconstruction

FIG. 4.3.   This is the same as the previous figure, except that the errors are now in the analysis of edge contrasts. The errors now propagate through the entire waveform, so that the reconstructed luminance at the start and finish are not the same.

argument applies to every point in the image: There is a series of different estimates of luminance. The general principle is that luminance difference is measured locally, but in reconstructing or representing the original signal, the effects of errors are propagated globally. Luminance difference is a *local measure*, brightness is a *global attribute*.

Exactly the same arguments would apply to the calculation of spatial location from location difference measurements, i.e. separations or distances between consecutive edges. The calculated position of any particular edge would depend on where the integrative reconstruction process began and what route it followed. It could begin, in parallel, at each edge in the array, so that the number of estimates of position for each edge would be the same as the number of edges involved. Each estimate would be equivalent to a measure of the distance from the edge in question to a different starting point. So how could the position of the edge be computed from all these different estimates?

The various estimates of position are placed about the real edge locus: The error in position for each estimate is the sum of all the individual separation errors between the starting point for that estimate and the edge in question. If all these errors are drawn from a distribution with zero mean and symmetric dispersion, then the mean of this distribution of estimates is a reliable, unbiased measure of the edge position. It can be seen that if the random error is drawn from a biased or skewed population, then this measure of position will itself be biased. If the mean of all estimates is taken as the computed position, then its reliability is uniform across the image and is determined by the standard deviation of the separation measurement errors, and the standard deviation of the errors introduced by the reconstruction process itself.

Constructing a One-dimensional Absolute Representation

Let us start with the primitive measurements, $_iS_{i+1}$, which are the estimates of the *separation* between adjacent edges i and $i+1$. If there are n edges, then there are $n-1$ such primitives. We can now calculate the separation, S, between any two edges j and k by adding up all the individual separations between them:

$$_jS_k = \sum_{i=j}^{k-1} {_iS_{i+1}} \qquad (j<k).$$

This quantity is equivalent to the *relative position*, $_jP_k$, of edge k with respect to edge j. If there are n edges in the image, then for any given edge k, there are n associated relative positions:

$$_1P_k \quad \cdots \quad _iP_k \quad \cdots \quad _nP_k.$$

Note that $_kP_k$ is a special case, and has the value 0.

It is now simple to impose a co-ordinate frame, by assigning an absolute position to one of the edges, edge m say. The *absolute position*, P_k, of any edge k is then obtained by adding the absolute position of edge m, P_m, to the relative position of edge k with respect to edge m:

$$P_k = P_m + {}_m P_k.$$

If each of the measurements of S has an error e, so that a particular measure s is related to the correct distance S by:

$$_i s = {}_i S + {}_i e$$

then the (long-range) separation of edges j and k will be calculated with an error, $_j e_k$, given by:

$$_j s'_k = \sum_{i=j}^{k-1} {}_i S_{i+1} + \sum_{i=j}^{k-1} {}_i e_{i+1}$$

$$_j e'_k = \sum_{i=j}^{k-1} {}_i e_{i+1}.$$

The prime on the s' and the e' indicates calculated quantities.

This is also the error in the relative position of edge k with respect to edge j.

Notice that the measures of relative position, including their errors, obey Euclidean geometry in that:

$$_j S'_k = {}_j S'_i + {}_i S'_k$$

and

$$_j e'_k = {}_j e'_i + {}_i e'_k.$$

In one dimension it is possible to specify that only separations between consecutive edges are measured, and that all other separations are inferred. This means that for any given edge declared as origin, all the other edges have determinate positions, because there is only one independent path from a given origin or starting point to each edge. Before we move on to consider the more interesting and valid two-dimensional case, let us just consider the effect of errors in a case where separations other than those between adjacent edges may also be measured. If the separation between edges j and k can be measured directly, with some independent error, then we can compare this measured separation $_jS_k$ with the calculated separation $_jS'_k$. In general, because all the measurement errors are independent, we have that:

$$_jS_k \neq {}^jS'_k$$

$$_jS_k \neq {}_jS'_i + {}_iS'_k$$

that is, that Euclidean geometry is not satisfied.

This means that the value for the absolute position of any given edge will depend on which route is taken, unless we constrain the measurements to be between adjacent edges only.

Constructing a Two-dimensional Absolute Representation

In two dimensions the measurements of the relationship between any two points as well as being expressed as two variables, separation and orientation, are less easily constrained. Consider three dots arranged so that they do not lie on a single straight line. We cannot now specify that only separations between adjacent dots are to be measured and thereby ensure that there is only one path for the reconstruction process to follow between any two dots. As a result, there will always be many different paths between any two dots, with as many estimates of their spatial relation. If the measurements are made with error then all these estimates will differ. In general, taking any one dot as origin, the computed position of any other dot will depend on the path taken to that dot, and so for any one starting point, there is a set of different estimates for the position of each other dot. This holds both for errors in the measurement primitives and those introduced subsequently in the calculation of relative positions.

What is the solution to this difficulty? In very general terms, the vector joining each dot to each other can be regarded as a constraint on the position of each dot. Any one of these constraints could be adjusted to approach a solution for the geometry of the dot layout. However, this will have implications for the positions of many other dots and may take the system further from a solution of some other point in the image. It is a bit like changing one spring in a bedstead. There is a rather generalised technique, known as *constraint relaxation*, that has been devised to help with situations like this. But relaxation is an iterative process and it imposes a time cost: The length of time taken to reach an acceptable solution will increase with the number of dots or elements involved, even for a parallel machine.

The process can be described along similar lines to the more formal argument employed in the one-dimensional case. Consider an irregular field of *n* scattered dots, on which, initially, a subset of all dot-pair relationships is measured and calibrated. The subset is perhaps selected according to some neighbourhood rule in the place of the sequential rule for the one-dimensional case, and is assumed to encapsulate all the necessary information. As before, it is necessary to complete the set of all dot-pair relationships; and since each spatial relationship is a vector, this is done with vector addition. Let us select out three dots, D_1, D_2, and D_3, from the field. These dots have their mutual spatial relationships specified by any two vectors, say $\overline{D_1D_2}$ and $\overline{D_2D_3}$, thereby leaving the final spatial relationship $\overline{D_1D_3}$ to be calculated by adding together the other vectors:

$$\overline{D_1D_3} = \overline{D_1D_2} + \overline{D_2D_3}.$$

There is no particular reasons for choosing dot D_2 as the intermediary between dots D_1 and D_3, and the vector $\overline{D_1D_3}$ could be calculated via other intermediaries:

$$\overline{D_1D_3} = \overline{D_1D_i} + \overline{D_iD_3} \qquad i = 1 \ldots n$$

leading to a set of n estimates of the vector $\overline{D_1D_3}$ (including the two degenerate cases when $i=1$ or 3). There is also a set of $(n)^2$ estimates of this vector obtained by adding three vectors, that is, by going from dot D_1 to dot D_3 via two intermediaries:

$$\overline{D_1D_3} = \overline{D_1D_i} + \overline{D_iD_j} + \overline{D_jD_3}$$

including the five degenerate cases of $i=1$, $i=3$, $i=j$, $j=1$, $j=3$. All possible paths of size $n-1$ or less from dot D_1 to dot D_3 form a set whose size is:

$$\sum_{i=0}^{n-1} (n)^i$$

including degenerate cases. If all degenerate cases are removed, then the set has size:

$$(n)^{n-1} - \sum_{i=0}^{n-2} (n)^i.$$

If each vector is measured with a particular error, then the various estimates will differ, and some form of weighted averaging process will be needed. The result at this stage is then the set of all dot-pair vectors $\overline{D_iD_j}$. This set still does not, in general, conform to the requirements of Euclidean geometry, because:

$$\overline{D_iD_j} \neq \overline{D_iD_k} + \overline{D_kD_j}$$

although the net error is now reduced. In a sense we could say that averaging the estimates of the vectors has involved the propagation through the image plane of the fundamental constraint of Euclidean geometry, although in this first pass the constraint has not been fully met. From the set of all current estimates of dot-pair vectors, a new value for each can be calculated by collecting all the indirect paths and averaging again. In fact, this iterative process could continue until the residual departure from Euclidean geometry was acceptable according to some predefined criterion. The number of iterations to reach this point will increase with n, which means that, degenerate cases excepted, the time to solve for the dot-pair vectors, which even in a parallel machine will depend on the number of iterations, will therefore be some monotonic increasing function of the dot number n.

This is an important result and the rest of this essay will be concerned with exploring its consequences for visual processing. A brief summary of the result and the conditions that forced it are thus in order. The calculation of the spatial position of a dot (I use dots, but more generally should consider intersections) or set of dots in an image requires an iterative process with the number of cycles increasing with the number of dots in the image (not just the number of dots whose positions are required). This is a time bottleneck that arises because the image position reconstruction requires extrapolation from position difference measurements, which are subject to errors. Precisely the same arguments should therefore apply to the other image quantity that is initially measured as differences, namely luminance/colour. In each case the difference measurements were statistically predictable in natural images, whereas the absolute measurements would not have been, and so calibration could only be guaranteed on the difference measures.

After calibration, some form of reconstruction process is required for two reasons: Only local spatial relationships are measured, so the more remote ones have to be computed; because of errors there is the need to propagate the vector addition constraint of Euclidean geometry through the image. This latter requirement gives rise to the constraint relaxation iterations, which constitute a time-consuming "bad step" or bottleneck.

We have to consider the dynamics of the process now. In machine vision, the sensor camera delivers a frame once every 40 ms or so, and if an implementation of the Primal Sketch could be guaranteed to have solved for position within this time, the system would be said to run in real time. The worst case is the largest n, which in machine vision is determined by the ratio of frame size to spatial resolution, and so given the time quantisation, the image size and spatial quantisation, and hardware speed characteristics, one could decide whether the system would ever fail in real time. In human vision, it is more difficult to reach such a decision. Time is not quantised in the same fashion, and the visual image changes continuously. The number of items per instant has an upper limit determined by the resolution of the system, but the time available to solve could in principle be infinitesimal. It seems likely that the Primal Sketch rate of processing in human vision could in principle be forced below real time, which would be disastrous. I now turn to ways in which this can be avoided.

GROUPING

Grouping is a word used by psychologists to discuss a selective association within a representation of certain elements of the description corresponding to certain features of a visual image. The features are usually spatially close together and have some common attributes: The letters in a word might be thought to be suitable for grouping together. Elements that lie in close proximity and share common attributes are likely to have a common physical cause or significance in the visual scene. They might, for example, all be textural markings on the same surface, in which case it can be deduced that the surface extends over the area. It is tempting to argue that the similarity between the texture markings should itself be explicitly represented. There is nothing in the output requirements for the Primal Sketch to indicate that this is necessary. The criterion is whether or not it is possible to devise a task that could only be done on the basis of representation of the grouping.

Grouping and Representation

Consider a flock of birds flying in a particular direction. Within the flock each individual has its own speed, direction, and altitude. The speed, direction, and altitude of the flock as a whole will be different but related to these individuals. In order to track the flock, it is necessary to calculate a mean speed, direction, and altitude from the individual behaviour of the birds. To accomplish this it is necessary to have a representation that allows the identification of what is a bird in that flock and what is not, but that is all. It is not actually necessary to create a representation in which membership of the flock is explicit. But what about the representation of the flock? Is this not a representation of a group? The answer is no. A representation that makes explicit the existence of the flock as a large object, moving at a particular speed, in a particular direction, and at a particular altitude, does not make explicit which birds are members of the flock. Even if some arbitrary task posed the question "is bird x a member of the flock?", it would be possible to decide on the relationship between the bird, as represented, and the flock as represented.

Consider the image of a tree and the reasons for creating a visual representation of it. We might wish to identify it as a tree, to recognise its species, to eat its fruit. We might wish to navigate around it, or perhaps hide behind it or in its branches. A representation of the shape, distance, and attitude of each visible leaf and the parts of the trunk and branches that were visible would be sufficient for all these purposes. There is no need to have a representation that explicitly recognises and records the similarities between the leaves. It is an interesting aside that Marr (1976) introduced grouping into his concept of the Primal Sketch (theta-aggregation, not curvilinear grouping, which is concerned with assessing edge continuity across pixels), but never needed it in his studies of stereopsis (Marr & Poggio, 1979), motion (Marr & Ullman, 1981), surface shape (Marr, 1977), or object representation (Marr & Nishihara, 1978).

Grouping in a representation is not essential to visual perception. I shall argue that grouping has a *computational* role, not a *representational* role. The introspective concepts in the minds of psychologists when treating grouping involve the general notion that representations should be economical, and that where patterns are found in nature, these can be used to compress the representation. Of course, repeating patterns in nature are often structural, and so they are useful in understanding the structure of the scene: The variations in texture across a surface are a powerful cue to depth variations across that surface (see Stevens, 1981). But grouping such patterns in a representation would render these variations implicit. Notwithstanding this, there is no justification for the more general principle of economical representation. The idea that sensory and perceptual systems must con- tinually act to reduce redundancy in representational stages is rooted in the vague notion that the machinery involved has a fixed and limiting size. The capacity of the brain, it is thought, has to be used at maximum economy, because it cannot be increased; it cannot be increased because of the size of the female pelvic outlet, etc. The argument has no firm axiomatic foundation.

Grouping and Computation

If explicit representation of grouping is not necessary, what does grouping exist for (assuming that it does exist)? The answer is that there is a computational need to restrict the number of elements that enter the process concerned with computing spatial positions, in order to achieve an accep- table speed of processing. If the visual system could aggregate local clusters of dots or whatever into groups and produce a spatial position solution (a *spatial metric*) for the groups as individual entities rather than for their component dots, then a first approximation to spatial layout could be computed much more rapidly. If we suppose that local measurements of local attributes of the *group* such as its shape can be made independently of the spatial metric process, then a significant step towards representing the image has been made. If we further suppose that non-spatial analysis of the dots within the group can also be made in parallel, then the resultant representation describes the location of the dot cluster, the overall layout of the cluster, and some statistical properties of the cluster such as the number of dots, their mean separation, etc. Although this representation is not complete in that the positions of the dots are not individually represented, it is a representation that can be computed much more rapidly than a full dot-by-dot description could be; and for many of the uses to which vision is put may well be sufficient.

There is a distinction here between usefulness or sufficiency and necessity. I have argued that a grouped representation is not strictly necessary; I am now suggesting that a grouped representation may be sufficient for certain visual tasks, provided that the grouping in the representation is concordant with the task. I am further suggesting that a grouped representation is preferable for considerations of processing time. Some visual tasks need only a partial representation: They will only require access to part of a full representation. An example is reading where the necessary information is the set and sequence of character identities. Spatial layout information in excess of the sequence (treating the space between words as a character) is not required; some aspects of the shape, size, orientation of the characters are not required. A computational grouping that initially delivered a partial representation that matched many task requirements would be valid and efficient.

The central requirement is a mechanism to produce the groups, and it would perhaps be sensible to seek some validity for the types of grouping achieved. Start by considering a mechanism that took the third letter of all five-letter words on this page and grouped those letters together. Such a mechanism would reduce the number of elements by one less than the number of five-letter words, but the idea sounds absurd. Representationally, it lacks validity because the grouping is orthogonal to the grouping that would be suitable for the task of reading. More important from the computational point of view, the position of the group with respect to other such groups does not reflect an approximate position for any element in the group, except fortuitously.

There would be a computational advantage derived from any type of grouping, if the number of iterations, N, to solve for spatial position was proportional to the number of elements, n, raised to any positive power:

$$N = (n-1)^a \quad a > 0.$$

Suppose that the n elements were grouped into m groups $(1 < m < n)$ each of n/m elements, and for argument that a had a value of 1. Without grouping, we have:

$$N = n - 1$$

with grouping, on the other hand, we have, for the processes between the groups:

$$N_g = m - 1.$$

For the elements within the groups, each group of which can be processed independently, and therefore in parallel, we have:

$$N_e = \left(\frac{n}{m} - 1 \right)$$

and so the total number of iterations is:

$$N = N_g + N_e = m - 1 + \frac{n}{m} - 1.$$

The condition for grouping to improve speed is then given by the requirement that this latter be smaller than $n - 1$:

$$m + \frac{n}{m} - 2 < n - 1$$

which is equivalent to:

$$m^2 - (n + 1)\, m + n < 0$$

from which we have:

$$(m - 1)\, (m - n) < 0$$

which leads to:

$$1 < m < n$$

which is the intention of the grouping process.

The grouping process can be nested hierarchically. Exactly the same argument would apply when considering the n/m elements within a group, within a group within a group, within a group within a group within a group, and so on.

This argument is powerful because it is about information processing in the abstract. Computationally speaking, any form of grouping gives a time advantage. It can be seen that the most efficient strategy in the abstract is to divide the total set of elements into subsets, or groups, or roughly equal sizes. We had:

$$N = m + \frac{n}{m} - 2.$$

The smallest value of N is obtained when m is equal to $n^{\frac{1}{2}}$.

This argument is quite independent of the way in which the different elements are assigned to the various groups: These arguments hold irrespective of the identities and relationships between the elements. Computationally, any form of grouping, nested or not, gives an improvement in processing speed, independent of any spatial considerations. Although no spatial aspects have been considered, there is an implicit need to do so. The grouping is most efficient when m equals the square root of n. If the rule had been that the optimum value of m was a fixed proportion of n, there would be no need to assess n: The optimum grouping of n would be achieved for an image with a relatively uniform distribution of elements simply by dividing the image into a fixed number of patches, each of which had an area that was in the same proportion to the area of the image as m should be to n. Each patch would have approximately the correct number of elements. But the rule suggests that the image be split down into a number of groups that depends on the square root of the number of elements in the image.

There is another, different way in which the grouping could be optimal. So far the advantages of grouping apply equally well when the grouping is not sensible, such as grouping the third letter of all five-letter words, or when the grouping is intuitively sensible, such as grouping together all the letters of each word. Why might this be sensible? If the Primal Sketch is rate-limited by a stage of spatial position analysis, it might sometimes be possible to skip over some of the deeper nested levels of position calculation without loss of performance for a particular task. This is much more likely to be true when the basis for determining what elements are grouped together is related to some constraints in natural images. One obvious and powerful constraint is that neighbouring parts of the image are more likely to be projected from close places in space than are remote parts of the image. A grouping that was based on the image proximity of elements would be efficient because the calculated position of the group could serve as an approximate measure of position for each of its member elements. Although there would be no representation of spatial relations between elements of the same group, other than that they were grouped and therefore neighbours, all other spatial relationships would be represented. To a first approximation, a spatial representation would have been computed.

Hierarchical Grouping

Grouping gives a speed advantage under two conditions. Generally, when the position of groups rather than elements is an acceptable approximation, there is a great benefit in grouping. Grouping also reduces the calculation time when the positions of elements are calculated only within separate groups. There is no interaction between elements of different groups, and the different groups are treated independently. This produces a hierarchical representation of position. Consider the representation of the relative positions of two dots in different groups. The relative positions of the two groups are known from the initial stage of calculation. The position of each dot with respect to its own group is known from the second stage of calculation. Therefore, the position of each dot with respect to the other is known, albeit indirectly. This is illustrated in Fig. 4.4. At the top of the figure

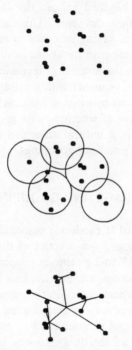

FIG. 4.4.   The effects of grouping on the calculation of position are illustrated. At the top is a field of randomly placed dots. Beneath this is an organisation of the dots into five groups. The positions of five groups can be calculated much more rapidly than the positions of 16 dots. At the bottom, a way in which the position of each dot can be represented hierarchically is suggested.

is a cluster of randomly placed dots. Immediately beneath this is drawn a potential grouping of the dots. Stage 1 would involve calculating the positions of these five groups. Stage 2 would involve calculating the position of each dot within its own group and with reference only to those other dots within the same group. The type of representation that arises is shown at the bottom of Fig. 4.4.

To give an idea of how effective this grouping might be let us suppose that the number of iterations per calculation is proportional to the number of dot dipoles. Sixteen dots will take *120* iterations. Five groups will take 10 iterations, and then a maximum of 6 dots per group takes a further 15, making a total of *25* iterations.

In the example of Fig. 4.4, all dots that fell within a specific distance of each other were grouped together. Suppose that we try the same trick again within each group, just by reducing the critical distance by, say, a factor of two. Obviously this can be repeated until there are no groups left with more than one element member. Figure 4.5 shows this taking place and the type of representation of space that develops. This time the total number of iterations is *17* at maximum, saving an order of magnitude!

Notice that the total number of iterations in different parts of the image varies. This is both because the number of levels in the hierarchy varies, and also because the number of elements within groups at any one level varies. This allows for asynchronous processing with each group being subdivided when it is ready, irrespective of whether other groups at the same level are ready. Notice that there is a natural structure to this hierarchy, always working from a large group to finer groupings.

MIRAGE AND GROUPING

Figure 4.6 shows a pattern of 16 randomly placed dark dots at the top, and in the centre, the zero-crossings from a series of different sized filters (space constants ranging from 0.35' to 2.8': the set proposed by Watt and Morgan, 1985). Although zero-crossings are not used as edge primitives, they are important as the places where each filter's signal is split into the two S signals. The largest filter produces an arch-shaped island of positive activity encompassing all the dots and surrounded by a moat of negative response. Smaller filters fail to link all the dots into one island of positive activity, producing instead a small number of distinct islands. The filters responses are shown as surfaces in Fig. 4.6a.

Of the various types of spatial structures in the random-dot pattern, there are clearly two extremes, corresponding respectively to the responses of the largest and the smallest filter. It is interesting to learn that MIRAGE preserves these two extremes, and none of the others, as can be seen in the

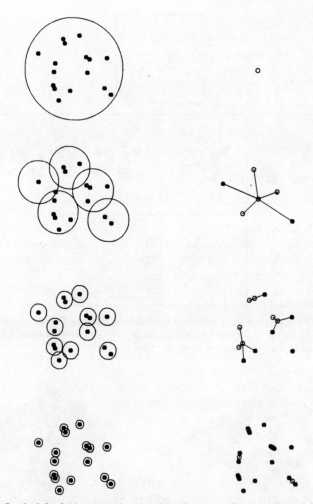

FIG. 4.5.   On the left of this column is a drawing of coarse to fine groupings of the dots from the same pattern as in Fig. 4.4. On the right a line skeleton indicates the two-dimensional tree structure that corresponds to the hierarchy of position representation.

bottom panel of Fig. 4.6, which shows two sets of zero-bounding contours. The positive signal, S^+, shown at the top in Fig. 4.6b, is a large, arched island covering all the dots; the negative signal, S^-, shown below is a blob-shaped island covering a larger area, but with holes in it where each of the dots was in the original image. The S^+ signal in this case is a reflection of the structure of the entire pattern of dots, and although it has local peaks on it where the dots are, the analysis of it in terms of its low-order central moments— perhaps like a medial axis transform—would not explicitly detect these. The

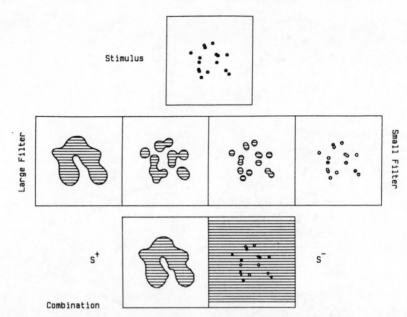

FIG. 4.6.   This figure shows a random field of 16 dots (at the top). Beneath this are the zero-crossings in the output of a range of different size second derivative Gaussian filters. At the bottom are shown the zero-bounding contours of the MIRAGE *S* signals.

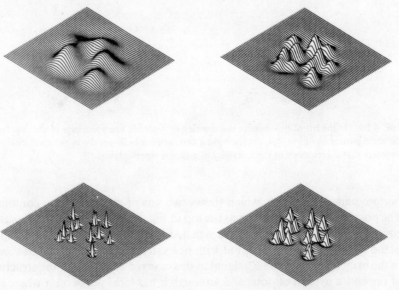

FIG. 4.6a.   The individual filter responses to the 16 random dots of Fig. 4.6. The largest filter is on the top left, and the smaller filters are then placed clockwise round from there.

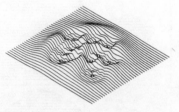

FIG. 4.6b.   This shows the S signals from the 16 randomly placed dots of Fig. 4.6. S^+ is on the top; S^- is on the bottom.

S^- signal, on the other hand, has little detail in it, except for its holes, and is a reflection of the space between the individual dots. If the dots had been bright on a dark background, then the roles of the S^+ and S^- signals would have been reversed.

The S^+ signal has only one zero-bounded island of response: It has found only one *element*. The S^- signal has marked the individual dots. In this way, the S^+ signal of MIRAGE can be said to have grouped all the dots together. Compare this with the desired grouping according to Fig. 4.5. MIRAGE has automatically discovered the largest range of grouping. How about the finer ones?

The individual filter responses in Fig. 4.6 are very close to the different levels of grouping in Fig. 4.5. The most effective way to access these individual filter responses through the MIRAGE operation is to switch off those filters whose size is greater than the level of grouping required. Figure 4.7 shows what happens when the filters are switched off in sequence, starting with the largest. Notice that the S^+ signals reveal in sequence the desired groupings.

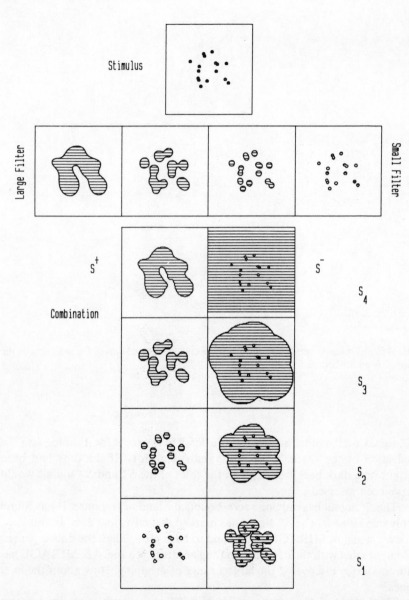

FIG. 4.7. This figure shows a random field of 16 dots (at the top). Beneath this are the zero-crossings in the output of a range of different size second derivative Gaussian filters. At the bottom are shown the zero-bounding contours of the MIRAGE S signals. S_4 refers to the result when all four filters are used; S_3 to the result when the smaller three only are used; S_2, the two smallest; S_1, the smallest alone. Notice how this use of the filter outputs provides the groupings as in Fig. 4.5.

100

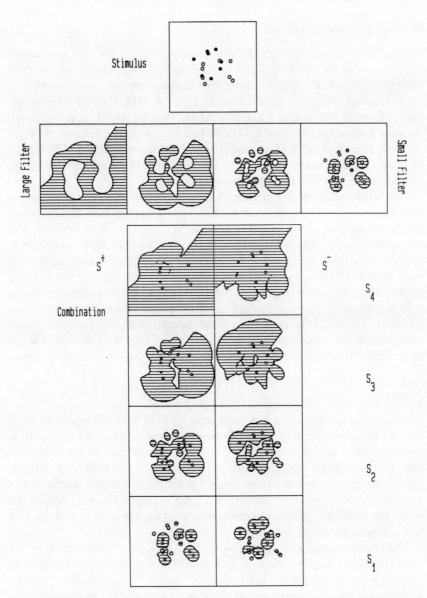

FIG. 4.8. This figure shows a random field of 16 dots (at the top), 8 of which are dark and 8 of which are light. Beneath these are the zero-crossings in the output of a range of different size second derivative filters. At the bottom are shown the zero-bounding contours of the MIRAGE *S* signals. Note how the different dot contrasts disrupts the grouping.

Dots of Different Contrasts

There are two variations on the random-dot pattern that are instructive. Suppose we select half of the dots at random and make them brighter than their background, leaving the other half darker than the background. The zero-crossings from the filter outputs, and the MIRAGE zero-bounding contours are shown in Fig. 4.8. It is apparent that MIRAGE does not group the dots together as effectively. If there had been a preponderance of bright or dark dots, then MIRAGE would have been more effective: The largest filter is basically summing light over a large area and responding to consistent trends away from the mean luminance.

The other variant on the random dots is the case where once again half the dots are darker and the other half lighter than the background, but this time, all the bright dots are on one side and the dark dots on the other side. The zero-crossings and the zero-bounding contours from MIRAGE are shown in the centre and bottom of Fig. 4.9 respectively. The figure shows that in this case, MIRAGE groups the two sets of dots quite separately. If the filters in MIRAGE were colour-opponent, then the system would group and segregate according to colour. This grouping behaviour is not unique to MIRAGE; it is merely the response of the largest filter. What is unique to MIRAGE is the preservation of the finest spatial scale (and no other) at the same time. MIRAGE can be said to automatically find these two extremes.

Lines

There are some oddities in the behaviour of MIRAGE. Figure 4.10 (top) shows a pattern of 8 random lines, formed from the original 16 random dots, and the zero-crossings arising from the lines (in the centre). At the bottom of Fig. 4.10 are shown the zero-bounding contours of the MIRAGE output, and it can be seen that the same general principle of extreme spatial scales applies. The S^+ signal now comprises a large island and a small island; the whole pattern is not grouped in this signal, even though it was when the dots had not been joined up into lines.

The important point illustrated by the lines example concerns the scope of what is loosely described so far as grouping. The line ends all lie at points in the image where there was a dot in the first example (Fig. 4.6). Even though all the dots were grouped in the S^+ signal, not all the lines are in this particular instance. This perhaps corresponds with vague intuitions and introspections about how grouping should treat the two images, but the lesson is that there is not a fixed distance within which any two visual items will group: It depends on what the items are, and what other contour is nearby.

The final example is based on a pattern of four overlapping random quadrilaterals, formed by pairing up the previous eight random lines. This

FIG. 4.8a. The individual filter responses to the 16 random dots of Fig. 4.8. The largest filter is on the top left, and the smaller filters are then placed clockwise round from there.

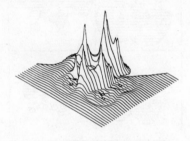

FIG. 4.8b. This shows the S signals from the 16 randomly placed dots of Fig. 4.8. S^+ is on the top; S^- is on the bottom.

103

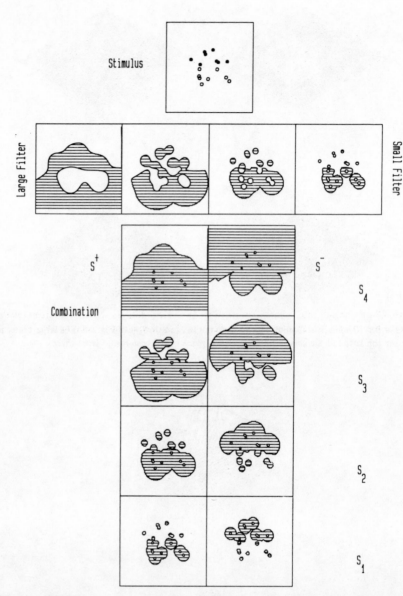

FIG. 4.9. This figure shows a random field of 16 dots (at the top), 8 of which are dark and 8 of which are light. Beneath these are the zero-crossings in the output of a range of different size second derivative filters. At the bottom are shown the zero-bounding contours of the MIRAGE S signals. Note how the different dot contrasts do not disrupt the grouping when they are segregated spatially.

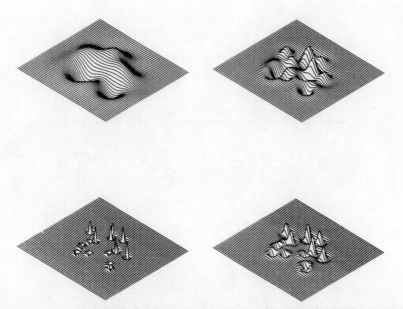

FIG. 4.9a.   The individual filter responses to the 16 random dots of Fig. 4.9. The largest filter is on the top left, and the smaller filters are then placed clockwise round from there.

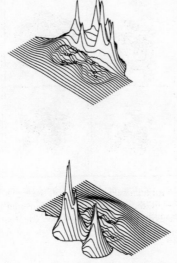

FIG. 4.9b.   This shows the S signals from the 16 randomly placed dots of Fig. 4.9. S^+ is on the top; S^- is on the bottom.

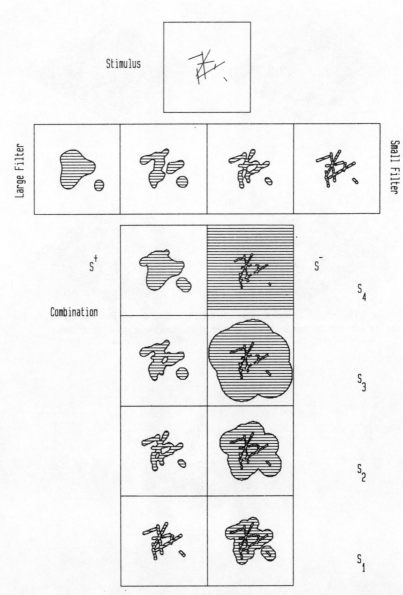

FIG. 4.10. This figure shows a random field of eight lines (at the top). Beneath this are the zero-crossings in the output of a range of different size second derivative Gaussian filters. At the bottom are shown the zero- bounding contours of the MIRAGE S signals.

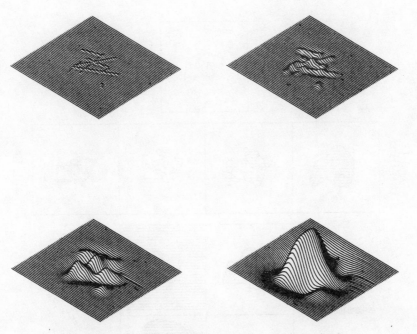

FIG. 4.10a. The individual filter responses to the lines stimulus.

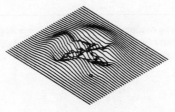

FIG. 4.10b. The S signals in response to the lines stimulus.

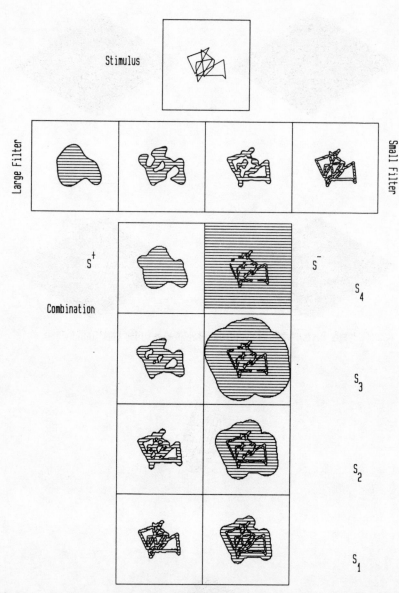

FIG. 4.11. This figure shows a random field of four quadrilaterals (at the top). Beneath this are the zero-crossings in the output of a range of different size second derivative Gaussian filters. At the bottom are shown the zero-bounding contours of the MIRAGE S signals.

FIG. 4.11a.   The individual filter responses to the quadrilaterals stimulus.

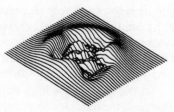

FIG. 4.11b.   The S signals in response to the quadrilaterals.

pattern and the zero-crossings that are to be found in the standard filter outputs are shown in Fig. 4.11. The pattern of zero-crossings is quite complex in this case and it is difficult to identify which is which in places. Notice how, just as at the end of the lines in the previous example, the zero-crossings tend to orbit round the corners at a larger distance from the image contour than where they are following a straight line (the distance is greater by a factor of $2^{\frac{1}{2}}$).

The bottom of Fig. 4.11 also shows the zero-bounding contours in the MIRAGE output. Not surprisingly, the S^+ signal groups all the contour, which in this instance is all connected together in the image. The S^- signal has holes in it, but they are not complete in the sense that not all the lines in the original are marked by holes here. Clearly it is not always true that MIRAGE automatically finds the two extremes of spatial scale.

A DYNAMIC MIRAGE

The general conclusion of the illustrations is that the MIRAGE operation produces two signals that between them contain a grouping of the contours as well as some information about the contours themselves. Previous discussion of grouping has led to a requirement that similar neighbouring contours be grouped together for the rapid computation of spatial position. The grouping requirement is at least in part met in the S signals of the MIRAGE transformation: Like elements and connected elements are grouped together, if they lie close enough to each other. Furthermore, the hierarchical grouping can be realised by a simple mechanism that sequentially switches off the outputs of the filters, starting with the largest and moving progressively through finer and finer scales.

This suggestion is shown schematically with a one-dimensional example in Fig. 4.12. At the top of the figure is a luminance waveform, which is a series of parallel bright lines whose luminance is modulated sinusoidally over a spatial period that is much longer than the interval between the lines (a stimulus used by Morgan and Watt, 1982). The lines themselves and the luminance modulation are two different spatial structures at different scales in the image but at the same location in space.

At the bottom of the figure is shown the consequence of switching out the output of the largest filter from the process that creates the S signals. As a result, these signals have very many more zero-bounded distributions of activity than before. There is now no overlap, and so all the response distributions are analysed and their spatial positions are all computed. Whereas previously the exact positions of the lines were not represented but the modulation was, in this case, the modulation is not explicitly represented but the positions and varying luminances of the lines are. Simply by

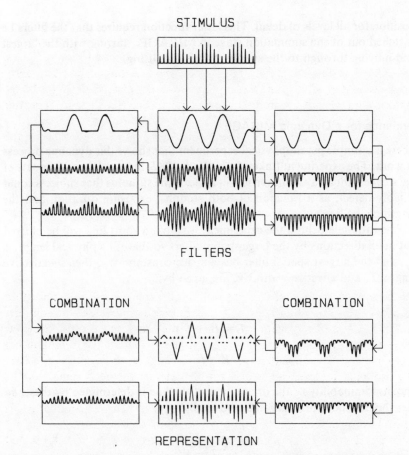

STIMULUS

FILTERS

COMBINATION   COMBINATION

REPRESENTATION

FIG. 4.12. The influence of f_n on the nature of the spatial representation that results from MIRAGE. At the top is shown the luminance profile of a stimulus, and beneath it, the responses of three different scale filters. The upper row of the combination stage is the case where all filter outputs are let into the S signals; the lower row shows what happens when only the two smaller filters are switched in. Notice how different the results are, and how many more elements there are in the latter case.

switching the largest filter's output in or out of the S signals, the system can determine the particular spatial scale that receives the position calculation. It is also determining how many elements the position calculation has to act upon. With the largest filter on, the position of the modulation is calculated; with it off, the positions of the individual lines are calculated.

Grouping thus has two interrelated purposes: (1) it allows a very rapid computation of spatial position for coarsely defined areas of the image with an associated parallel non-spatial analysis of finer detail; (2) it also provides the basis for a progressive, spatial scale, hierarchical computation of spatial position for all levels of detail. This latter function requires that the filters be switched out of the summation stage in MIRAGE, starting with the largest and moving through to the smallest, time permitting.

Evidence for a Dynamic MIRAGE

There is a simple psychophysical experiment that shows this dynamic process at work. The experiment (taken from Watt, 1987) involved measurements of the smallest tilt away from vertical in a short-line stimulus that subjects could reliably detect, as a function of both stimulus exposure duration and the length of the line.

The rationale behind the experiment was that a short line will be blurred out in all directions by the large spatial filters so that if its physical length is L_p, and the largest spatial filter has a space constant of f, then its effective length, L, and effective width, W, are given by:

$$L=(L_p{}^2+f^2)^{\frac{1}{2}}$$

$$W=f.$$

The discriminability of the orientation of the line is determined by these, so that the threshold orientation θ is given by:

$$\theta^2 = k^2\frac{L^2}{L^2-W^2}$$

$$\theta = k\frac{(L_p{}^2+f^2)^{\frac{1}{2}}}{L_p} = k(1+f^2/L_p{}^2)^{\frac{1}{2}}.$$

Thus the orientation threshold is determined by the ratio of L_p to f. Figure 4.13 shows the variation of orientation threshold with L for three exposure durations, of 35 ms, 100 ms, and 500 ms. Also drawn on the figure as continuous functions are the predicted variations for different values of f. At 35 ms, the value of f is about 1 arc degree; at 100 ms, it is about 16 arc min; and at 500 ms, it is about 4 arc min. This behaviour is exactly what is expected if the dynamic change of spatial scale is taking place.

In a comparison experiment, Watt (1987) measured the time course of visual resolution. This did not vary with stimulus exposure, indicating that the finest spatial scales are available at all times, but only for the texture type of discriminations.

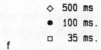

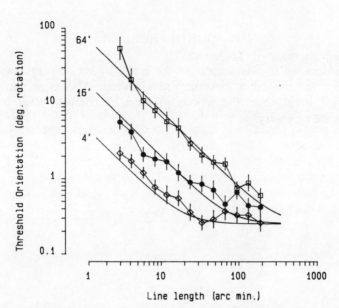

FIG. 4.13. The variation of orientation threshold with line length and exposure duration. The continuous functions are derived in the text. The point illustrated is that as exposure duration increases, the value of f, the largest filter space constant in use decreases.

SUMMARY

The discussion of how spatial position is calculated has identified a computational step where the speed of the Primal Sketch is limited by the number of elements it has to process. This rate-limiting process arises because the system makes measurements of spatial differences (separation) not spatial positions. These in turn were made because the former may be automatically calibrated, unlike the latter.

Spatial position, and by an analogous argument, luminance/colour, is then reconstructed by an iterative process that takes longer the more elements that are involved. Time can be saved by arbitrary grouping into a hierarchy, but more importantly, if the grouping is sensible, then some steps in the hierarchical computation of position can be skipped. A few examples of how MIRAGE groups parts of images have been discussed. In general, MIRAGE seems a valid way of grouping the image, although it has a few anomalies.

Finally, it has been demonstrated that a hierarchy of grouping levels can be created by the simple process of switching off filters prior to summation into the S signals. The sequence of switching off should move from coarse to fine spatial scales in order.

THE FOURTH PROBLEM

We have been led in this chapter of the essay, by way of argument and experiment, to consider a dynamic Primal Sketch. This is an intriguing possibility, but it raises the serious problem of control. What control processes are necessary?

5 Control of Primal Sketch Processing

Grouping has been described as a tool that allows the calculation of spatial positions to proceed rapidly. MIRAGE has been shown to have a property of grouping due to the behaviour of its largest spatial filter. This grouping is generally sensible, so that, for example, a cluster of dots that lie close together are represented as a single group. At the same time as the group is formed, some detail is preserved in the S signals. The position of the group is calculated along with its overall shape and some statistical measures of the details. This leaves the positions of the dots themselves not represented explicitly or implicitly: The representation is partial. How could it be made complete?

The visual system cannot just go and solve the spatial position of the dots of a group with respect to the group position because the output of MIRAGE lacks any primitive response distributions corresponding to the individual dots. In the present example, their presence is indicated only by holes in the negative response. Figure 5.1 shows what happens to the zero-bounded contours of the MIRAGE output as the larger spatial filters are progressively turned off, which is equivalent to decreasing the one free parameter of MIRAGE, f_n, the space constant of the largest filter. The large group is replaced by increasingly finer groups until eventually each resolvable dot is distinct (in this case when only the smallest filter is active). At each stage in this progression it is proposed that the groups are analysed for spatial position with reference to the group at a larger scale at the same place in the previous step of the progression. Gradually, the representation of

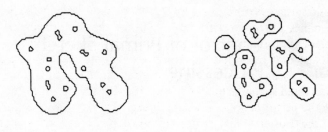

FIG. 5.1. This figure shows the zero-bounding contours of the MIRAGE S signals for the 16 randomly placed dots of Fig. 4.7. At the top left are the contours as shown in that figure, and moving clockwise from this are the contours that result when the filters are progressively switched out. Notice how the number of groups increases.

spatial position is refined according to a natural hierarchy that is as much determined by the image as by the process.

GROUPING AND TEXTURE

Texture was the original reason for incorporating spatial filters of various sizes into the Primal Sketch. The need to maintain some form of representation of the finest scales was the reason for combining the outputs from spatial filters of different sizes. Clearly, where the local microstructure of a pattern is repeated over a surface, like the leaves on a tree, there is only a small, perhaps insignificant, benefit for many aspects of the behaviour of an organism in identifying where each local element is. Given the previous argument about time considerations in computing position information, there would be some advantage in treating repetitive patterns statistically as texture.

Recall Fig. 2.7. The luminance waveform in Fig. 2.7 is derived from textured surfaces, and the output of MIRAGE reflects the two different spatial scales, which correspond roughly to surface discontinuities and creases, and surface texture markings. Although the hierarchy of spatial scale that determines a precedence for large spatial scales was introduced because of the abstract information-processing constraints discussed in the previous section, it also may categorise the information into primary surface discontinuities (= large scale) and secondary texture (= small scale). The discontinuities are processed spatially, but the texture is processed only statistically. This is exactly the performance one would desire.

Kahn and Foster (1981) performed an experiment that is particularly interesting in this respect. They briefly presented to subjects two patterns, right and left of fixation, each comprising seven randomly placed dots. Subjects were asked to judge whether the two patterns were totally different, or the same except for a rotation, dilation, or reflection. Accuracy of responses was measured, and varied according to condition, and also according to whether the two patterns were symmetrically placed about fixation or not. In order to account for the results, Kahn and Foster proposed the separate encoding of local spatial relations (within a pattern) and global spatial relations (between patterns, with respect to the point of fixation). These two correspond well with the hierarchical representation outlined in this present section.

Texture Segregation

The boundaries between textures that have different forms are obviously very important. The properties of texture that allow such boundaries to be seen, i.e. that allow different textures to be segregated, have been studied widely. There is a great difference between the types of textures found in the environment and those created for experimental purposes. The latter comprise a regular or nearly regular array of identical or nearly identical subpatterns. The sub-patterns themselves are usually made of lines and dots. There is a vast literature on the discrimination of such texture patterns, and a comprehensive review would be beyond the scope of this work. However, there are several general principles that can be stated in the present context. The discrimination of texture differences involves creating a representation of the boundary of each texture patch. This in turn relies on detecting the different characteristics of the two patches.

A very general finding is that some patterns may be distinguished very rapidly, whereas others require detailed scrutiny. These may be discrete categories derived from the operations of different mechanisms or the creation of different representations. They may also represent two extremes of a continuum. There is little data available to support either, although this thought experiment favours the continuum: A pair of texture patterns made of lines that differ by a factor of 2 in length will be more readily and rapidly discriminated than two that differ by a factor of 1.02, even though in each case the difference is line length. It is not enough to say that line-length texture differences can be discriminated effortlessly or pre-attentively.

Julesz (1981) has argued that textures with different first-order statistics (distributions of grey-levels) or different second-order statistics (distributions of pairs of grey-levels) can be effortlessly discriminated. All other patterns can only be discriminated with effort, except for cases where the distribution of special features, *textons*, is different. The textons include line ends, and perhaps corners and intersections as well.

The boundaries between patterns with different first-order statistics (especially mean luminance) are detected by spatial filters that are large enough not to resolve the sub-patterns themselves. MIRAGE will be able to segregate such patterns. For the other types of texture differences, the MIRAGE operation does not necessarily segregate the textures.

Characterising Textures

The subject of how textures might be characterised is vast. I shall draw attention to just one small aspect of the subject, which is important for the ideas of control that follow.

The response of a large filter to a patch of uniform texture, such as that in Fig. 1.11, is not readily distinguishable from its response to a uniform grey patch. The response of a small filter, on the other hand, obviously is different in the two cases. The consequence of this is that the S signals that arise from the texture are both different from the equivalent S signals arising from an uniform grey patch. Figure 5.2 shows two such S signals. Compared with the response of a single large filter, shown in Fig. 5.3, they have two distinctive characteristics. Notice that the S^- signal (in this case) has response activity over the area of the texture and that this activity has small holes in it where the signal is at zero. Notice also that the S^+ signal has response activity over the area of the texture and that this has a large number of spikey peaks.

The frequency of different values within the two relevant zero-bounded response distributions is therefore quite different in the texture case from the uniform grey field case. This could potentially provide a powerful, characteristic descriptor of the texture.

The S signals that arise from textures made up of lines are also interesting in a similar fashion. Re-examining Figs. 4.6 to 4.11 shows that the shape of the holes in S^- provide some information about the texture elements. (Remember it is only S^- because the patterns are dark-on-light.) The possibility exists that some information about number of dots, corners, etc. could be retrieved, even though the position of such configurations would not be known.

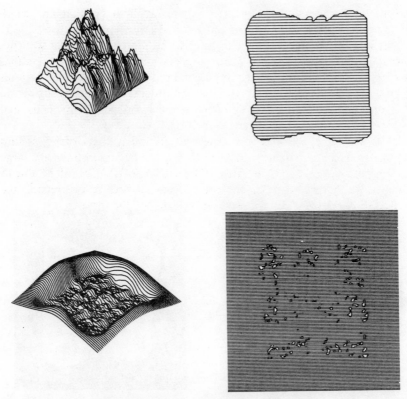

FIG. 5.2.   The S signals that derive from the patch of texture shown in Fig. 1.11.

THE TIME SEQUENCE OF AUTOMATIC PROCESSING

The number of elements at any particular spatial scale is not predictable other than within fairly tolerant limits. The coarsest useful spatial scale in the image is also not predictable, and so the initial number of elements in the spatial analysis can vary widely. Therefore it follows that the time after image onset that the process of filter switching should start is determined by the content of the image. There is a need for feedback control and asynchronous processing rather than a strict and uncontrolled sequence of processing. There must be substantial dynamic memory (dynamic memory is perfectly erasable) so that the state of the system throughout the control cycles can be preserved. It is worthwhile considering how this control process invoked over MIRAGE might work and what requirements it has. It could simply be an automatic process, initiated and executed independently in different regions of the visual field, or it could be governed by high-level considerations.

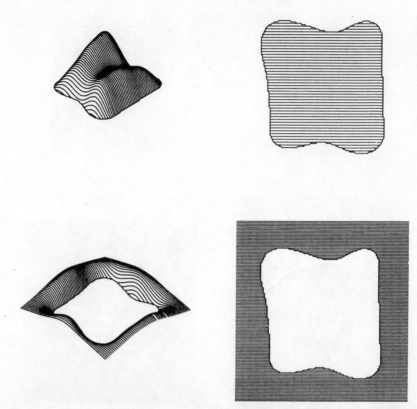

FIG. 5.3.   The response of the largest filter to the texture patch of Fig. 1.11. The response is drawn in the same format as Fig. 5.2 for comparison. Notice how the texture manifests itself in the complete MIRAGE output.

Initial Response to Change

The filters themselves are continuously active at all points in the visual field. There exist switches on their outputs that control whether or not these are added into the S signals. A change in the visual stimulus at any point immediately causes corresponding changes in the filter outputs.

Suppose that there is some steady-state image in the visual field that has been present long enough for most of the filters to have been switched out of the summation step. Then a change in the image occurs, and so the responses of filters around about the point where the change occurred are also changed. Automatically that portion of each filter's response that has changed is allowed through to the summation step: Over the area in which a filter has changed its output, that filter is switched into the summation. Automatically

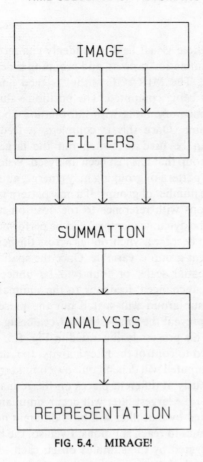

FIG. 5.4.   MIRAGE!

switching in of filters according to this rule will usually cause all of the filters to be switched in at that point. For a point that is distant from a change by a distance d, all filters with space constants greater than about $2d$ will be switched into the summation step. The further away from the change a point is, the smaller the range of the filter size that will be switched in.

Notice that there is an implied control signal in the filters. When a filter's output changes at a specific location in the image, both the new value and the fact that this is a new value have to be signalled. This control signal would be a transient, boolean, positive feedforward signal. It would have to be transient to avoid holding the system at its reset condition for too long. Its effect would be all-or-none, switching the new value into the summation step.

Processing Cycle

Suppose that the whole visual field is suddenly changed. All the filters are switched into the summation process, and grouping is determined by the size of the largest filter. The MIRAGE output is then analysed, with spatial position for groups being computed. The position value for each group is stored in dynamic memory along with information about the largest filter size at the same time. Once this is complete, a feedback signal to the summation step can be used to switch out the largest filter within the boundary of each group that has just been analysed. When the largest filter is switched out, a new pattern of grouping may emerge, and would be indicated by an increase in the number of groups. If a new pattern is found, then spatial position computations with reference to the position of the parent group (which is stored in the dynamic memory) can be performed. Note that at this point processing can become asynchronous across the field, as the number of sub-groups per parent group is variable. Once the spatial solution has been obtained at this spatial scale, or found to be unnecessary because the grouping pattern is unchanged, feedback to the summation step within the boundary of each sub-group will switch out the present largest filter. A terminating rule to prevent the smallest filter from being switched out would also be necessary. This process is illustrated in Fig. 5.5.

If feedback is used to control the filter activity, the rate at which the final representation is computed will depend on how complex the scene is, and will proceed asynchronously at different places on the retinal image. The initial step of switching out the largest filter will occur simultaneously everywhere, but the groups created by that filter will have different numbers of elements and thus different times to reach solutions. Even so, the process is effectively automatic: It is triggered by the stimulus onset; each filter is switched out when the previous calculations are complete; and the process terminates when there are no remaining groups, just single elements. This would be when the structure of S^+ and S^- are complementary.

The representation of spatial position that is produced is hierarchical, with the position of an element referred upwards to the next larger-scale group and so on, to the largest scale. Although there is no need to record the range of filters that were switched into the summation step for each level in this representation hierarchy in order to be able to interpret spatial position, if the image changes, such a record would make it possible to avoid restarting the whole process over the whole field.

In this discussion so far of the control of the size of the largest filter at different places in the image, the possibility of entirely automatic control has been stressed. There are several observations that should be noted. The control mechanism, switching out or in filter responses, is simple and therefore reliable. The spatial area over which it is done is determined by the

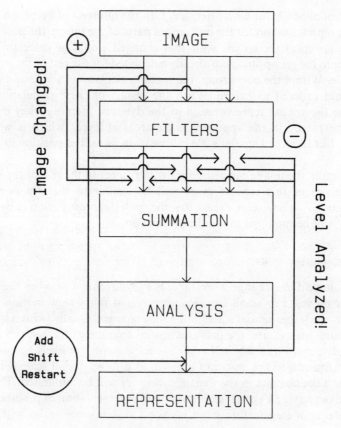

FIG. 5.5.   MIRAGE with control signals.

zero-bounded distributions of the groups in the current S signals. The timing of control is determined by the rate of the position calculations, and changes in the stimulus. The results are stored in dynamic memory in a natural structured order, which is particularly appropriate for modifications when new items enter the field, items move within the field, or the observer and eyes move. Although many details are left implicit, there is a self-organising aspect to this control that matches the self-calibrating behaviour described in the previous section.

Types of Image Change

Consider what happens when a dot is added to the image. All the filters around the point where the dot appeared change their activity, out to a distance of about $2f$ for each filter size, f. In the interests of keeping a stable position representation for the unchanged parts of the image, the position of the new group at the largest scale that changed would be calculated with reference to the group structure already calculated for the rest of the image at that scale. Within the new group, the spatial calculations would all be new, but would proceed as before. When the results of these calculations are added to the spatial representation in the dynamic memory, they must of course be placed in the appropriate hierarchical levels, which is why the memory has to record spatial scale information as well as position information.

An item in the image can also move with respect to the rest of the image. The analysis of this type of event will be similar to that following the introduction of a new item, except that the spatial representation in dynamic memory will be modified in a different fashion.

Eye Movements

The whole field can change when there is eye movement or when the whole observer moves. For small eye movements, and fairly slow motion of the observer, the larger spatial scales will not be changed greatly (with respect to their spatial scales), and the previous spatial solution at these scales can be used with a small translation. Larger eye movements are likely to move the point of fixation to the centre of a group at a large spatial scale (Findlay, 1982), and the changes in the dynamic memory will be minimised. This is a benefit from having a spatial scale structured representation of position. This can be taken a step further if we invoke a stability constraint within the calculation of the representation.

Suppose that the eye moves to the centroid of one of the groups in the largest spatial scale and that no other changes in the retinal image occur. All the largest groups have moved, and all by the same amount in terms of visual angle. The representation in dynamic memory, which at this top level was with respect to an arbitrary group, thus has not changed, provided it is known what the movement was.

Provided that the dynamic memory representation is in a geometry that corresponds to the scene, rather than a retinal geometry, nothing has changed. So why move the eye? The central fovea has a finer resolution than the periphery of the visual field, and it is therefore capable of producing a deeper hierarchical representation. If the position of the fovea can be aligned with some large-scale group in the current representation, then this current representation can be updated relatively rapidly by the addition of some extra sentences.

It is interesting that when subjects are asked to move their eyes to one of several peripheral targets, they tend to saccade first to a point central to all the targets and then on, or back to, the particular target (Coren & Hoenig, 1972; Findlay, 1982).

By treating the entire visual system, including eye movements, in this way, it is possible to describe it as a single system.

PSYCHOLOGICAL EXPERIMENTS ON AUTOMATIC PROCESSING

Generally, psychological experiments in visual perception lack the quantitative details that allow psychophysics, for example, to discover the mechanisms of vision. Bearing this stricture in mind, there are some experiments that may be interpreted in the terms of this essay. This is rather different from the usual ways in which the experiments have generally been treated. For this reason alone they are included.

The Time Course of UnGrouping (a)

A prototypical experimental design is that of Treisman and Gelade (1980), who displayed an array of visual stimuli to subjects and asked for a decision about the presence or absence of a particularly defined target within that array. The target could be defined by a single feature that distinguished it from all others in the display array, or it could be the conjunction of two critical features, each of which appeared separately in the array as well. The features used were distinctive colours and/or letter identities, the independent variable was number of stimulus elements in the array, and the dependent measure was search time.

The basic findings are illustrated in Fig. 5.6 and were that:

1. Time taken to detect the presence of a target specified by a single distinguishing feature did not vary with array size.
2. Time taken to discover the target's absence increased with the number of stimulus elements, when the target was specified by a single feature.
3. Time taken to detect the presence of a target specified by a feature conjunction increased with array size.
4. Time taken to discover the target's absence when the target specification was the conjunction of two distinguishing features was twice as long as the time to discover the same target's presence.

The authors show how these results can be accounted for by the proposition that detecting a single feature's existence requires no time-consuming serial processing, but that the array elements must be processed one after another in order to discover whether a feature conjunction exists.

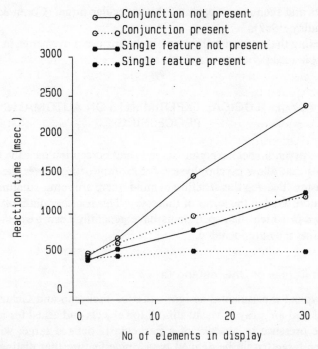

FIG. 5.6.   The time taken for subjects to decide whether a particular target is present in a display or not, as a function of display size. The data are taken from Fig. 1 of Treisman and Gelade (1980).

The serial process is necessary to bring together the different feature attributes of each element. Within the framework of the theory of Primal Sketch visual processing that has been described in this essay, a somewhat different deduction follows. I take the findings in sequence.

The first two findings simply define the discriminability of a blue letter T or X, or a green or brown S from an array of green Xs and brown Ts. The absence of an effect on search time when the target was present is due to the unique feature, blueness or curvilinearity without contour intersections, being available in the initial representation. Colour is represented because if the filters have some colour-opponency, then the initial grouping will reflect colour differences; intersections and contour shape are also represented as described on p. 116.

Now, turn to the third and fourth findings. The conjunction of two different distinguishing features in one single target element is defined as a spatial coincidence. This means that spatial-position information has to be computed for the judgement to be made. Even with parallel processing, this takes more time the more elements there are in the array. If we are a little more rigorous in describing this, the reason for a difference in the time to detect the presence or absence of the feature conjunction target will be clear.

Half the elements in the display are brown Ts, half are green Xs, and they are randomly intermixed; the target is a green T. Since the filters are colour-opponent, the initial grouping on the stimulus array will be rather like that shown for random dots in Fig. 4.8: There will be a number of separate green groups, each comprising of one, two, three, or more elements. Occasionally the target will be in a one-member group, and so its position and therefore feature conjunction are known immediately. When it is in a larger group, the fact that it is a T and not an X will be much less apparent, and so the group will have to be broken down by switching off the largest filter. It can be seen that rarely will the whole hierarchy of groups need to be broken down before a positive identification can be made, but always before a negative identification. Hence the difference in response times in these two cases.

This argument is rather analogous to that offered by Treisman and Gelade, but differs in that they supposed serial search across visual space at the finest spatial scale, whereas the present argument supposes parallel search across visual space at each spatial scale, but a sequential progression from large spatial scales towards the finest. It is relevant to note that in the feature conjunction search, where spatial position has to be computed for the target, subjects were able to locate the target correctly; but when a single feature was sought, and so spatial position need not be computed, subjects were able to identify where the target was on only 60% of trials.

The Time Course of UnGrouping (b)

Another type of experiment that shows the process of undoing grouping was carried out by Eriksen and Eriksen (1974). Subjects were shown a target capital letter $\frac{1}{2}$ arc degree across and asked to categorise it as being from one of two predefined sets. On either side of the target there was a string of three flanking irrelevant letters. The two target sets were $\langle H,K \rangle$ and $\langle S,C \rangle$, i.e. letters made of straight line segments with intersections versus letters made of curvilinear segments with no intersections. The flanking letters were either from the same target set (compatible response), the alternative target set (incompatible response), or from neither target set. In this case the flanking letters could be similar to the target or dissimilar.

The basic finding was that the flanking letters made response slower provided that they lay less than about 1 arc degree from the target (edge-to-edge). The extent of response slowing is shown in Fig. 5.7 and may be summarised as follows:

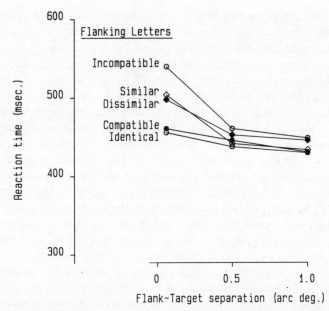

FIG. 5.7.   The time taken for subjects to decide to which of two predefined categories a target letter at the centre of a line of letters belongs. Details are given in the text. The data are taken from Fig. 1 of Eriksen and Eriksen (1974).

1. Slowest response for flanking letters that required an incompatible response, e.g. to an H surrounded by Ss.
2. Rather less slowing with flanking letters that belonged to neither response category. Within this case, there was a small effect of whether the flanking letters were similar to the target or not, with the latter case being a little slower.
3. There was very little response slowing with flanking letters that were the same as the target or that required a compatible response.

In each case the response slowing is with respect to a single, unflanked target control condition. In all cases the response slowing monotonically reduces with increasing separation between target and flanks. At a separation of 1 arc degree the incompatible response and dissimilar but not categorised letters had the same effect, but no other condition did.

The general type of explanation in the terms of this essay for this finding is that responses are based on the presence or absence of intersections in the letters. When a large spatial scale group comprising all three letters contains members of each category, response is slowed because the group has to be broken down to identify the letter locations so that the central letter can be examined. Targets $\langle H,K \rangle$ both have intersections, whereas targets $\langle S,C \rangle$ do not. The letters chosen from neither category were $\langle N,W,Z \rangle$ and $\langle G,J,Q \rangle$, which were designed to be visually similar to the groups $\langle H,K \rangle$ and $\langle S,C \rangle$ respectively. At 30 arc min. separation, the dissimilar case slows response by almost as much as an incompatible-response letter (i.e. Q slows response to K almost as much as H does), but similar letters have little or no effect (N does not affect response to K). Similarity behaves the same as membership of the compatible-response class, and dissimilarity behaves the same as membership of the incompatible-response class, where class membership is determined by the presence or absence of line intersections. Note that one of the neither-category sets, $\langle G,J,Q \rangle$, has intersections but the intersecting line segments are very small and will probably not be resolved except when close to the fovea. When these flanking letters were 3.75 arc min. from the target, they will all ($\langle N,W,Z \rangle$ and $\langle G,J,Q \rangle$) have behaved as if they were similar to $\langle H,K \rangle$ and dissimilar to $\langle S,C \rangle$; whereas further away, the two sets $\langle N,W,Z \rangle$ and $\langle G,J,Q \rangle$ would be more likely to map in similarity onto the sets $\langle H,K \rangle$ and $\langle S,C \rangle$ respectively, as the authors intended. At the closest spacing there should be no difference between similar and dissimilar, in each case a half-strength effect is expected because half of the letters classified as similar were actually dissimilar, according to their intersections, and vice versa. Over a series of trials, a half-strength effect will average out. This is exactly what was obtained at 3.75 arc min. separation.

The general conclusion, given this treatment of letter similarity in terms of intersections, is that irrelevant flanking letters slow response if they are of the opposite category (intersections vs. no intersection), and that this effect reduces monotonically with increasing separation. If the letters are grouped together, then their individual spatial positions are not represented, and a response is possible only if all letters indicate the same category. If the group of stimulus letters indicates both response categories, then a response is not indicated by the initial representation. The position of the various letters must be calculated to reveal the central letter. This means that the largest filters have to be switched out, reducing f_n until the individual letters are resolved by the largest filter still active. This will take time, and more time the smaller the resolution distance. The findings of Eriksen and Eriksen are thus seen to match the general theory of the control and dynamics of the Primal Sketch elaborated in this essay.

CONTROL BY DELIBERATE INTERVENTION

Control of the nature of the Primal Sketch representation by a time-extended process with simple feedback is an attractive suggestion. The start condition is image change, and the termination condition is either a subsequent image change causing a reset or the point where no grouped structure still remains unexplored in the representation.

If the feedback process could itself be governed by higher-level goals, then a considerable degree of flexibility to match time available for processing to depth of processing would be possible. The most obvious form of control concerns eye movements. Because the finest spatial resolution of the eye is at its centre, the fovea, it is necessary to move the eye from place to place in the scene to make available all the fine detail. The time at which the eye moves is determined by the visual system: Either it has completed the representation of the current foveal part of the image, or the construction of a full representation is interrupted when something potentially important changes in the scene and requires examination.

Suppose, for example, a line of text is being read. The higher-level government has to control eye position on the basis of word layout (the gaps in the line), and has to control the visual processes required for word recognition. Word recognition clearly involves higher-level knowledge of a definition for each word and letter of the visual pattern expected. That knowledge may itself have a hierarchial spatial structure. Suppose that a common word like "THE" has a full definition of letter shapes, order, and spacing, but also has partial definitions that omit spatial terms like letter order. Letter shape definitions can be relatively full in terms of primitive features (corners, line ends, etc.) and their spatial relations; or the shape definitions can be partial, perhaps only a list of primitive features from the set of corners, intersections, and line ends.

To match an input word image to the full recognition definition would require full spatial processing, with the attendant cost in time spent. On the other hand, if the high-level process had context information and could generate a small set of expectations that it wanted to discriminate between, their partial definitions may be sufficient; in which case, the spatial position calculation process could be terminated at the point where the entire word was a group. At this juncture, word outline shape and size are represented, and a statistical representation of the primitive features is also available. This could match one of the partial word definitions, and the eyes could then be moved to the next word very rapidly.

Thus time can be saved where appropriate by setting the termination condition on a process. There is another simple way in which high-level government can control the feedback process, by setting the starting condition. Suppose that you were to set yourself the task of counting the number of vowels in the first word of this sentence. You know both the average size and average spacing of letters for this type of print, and you can easily locate the word in question. The task is difficult enough that you are likely to do it visually rather than from memory, and is predictable enough for it to be unnecessary to use all the larger-scale groupings. It might make sense, in this case where a representation of much of the scene has already been computed, to use only a relatively fine scale, to set the starting value of f_n low, compared with its value if you were required to count the number of words on that line.

The important point here is that low-level automatic control of the size of the largest filter in use is a simple one-parameter feedback process, and higher-level control of that feedback is also a simple one-parameter process setting the termination condition. These two levels of control could each be implemented in parallel across the visual field. Examples of this high-level control in action are provided by two other types of psychological experiments as will now be described.

Selection of Initial Spatial Scale (a)

Posner et al. (1980) reported that the latency for the simple detection of the sudden appearance of a small spot of light could be reduced by providing an indication to the subject of where it would appear. This potential accele-ration of response soon fades if the target does not appear, and after a few hundred milliseconds, response latency will increase so that subjects are slower than they would be if the information had not been provided (Maylor, 1985). This delay of response also fades after a further period. The phenome-non is illustrated in Fig. 5.8. The effect of acceleration followed by a slowing of response has a closely analogous effect to the changes in the threshold intensity for a spot of light (Bashinski & Bacharach, 1980) that follow an attentional instruction. This finding implies that a low-level visual task can be influenced by events that precede the stimulus and that may bear only a semantic relationship to the task. The details of this finding follow from a consideration of first, how the sensitivity to a small dot depends on the size of the largest active filter, and second, how this size varies after the attentional instruction is received.

It is assumed that response latency is a monotonic function of signal strength in a simple detection task, hence the equivalence of latency and sensitivity results. Therefore, the finding would be explained if it could be shown that the signal-to-noise strength for a given luminance spot increased above normal after the instructions, fell back to normal, reduced below normal, and then rose back to normal again. What changes in the size of the filters that were switched into the S signals would produce this trend?

There are two opposing effects relating signal-to-noise ratio to the size of the largest active filter in the case of a spot target. As the filter size increases, the effects of noise are reduced: The noise is averaged over a larger area. This will tend to increase signal-to-noise ratio in proportion to the square root of the filter area, that is, in proportion to the filter size. At the same time however, the signal itself is also spread out over an increasingly large area and is thus weakened in proportion to the square of the filter size. This means

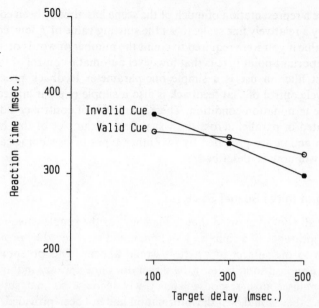

FIG. 5.8.   The time taken for subjects to detect the appearance of a spot of light in one of two predefined places. Valid trials were when the subject was cued to the correct location in advance; invalid trials were when the cue was to the wrong location. Target delay is measured from the time of the cue. The data are taken from Fig. 9.1 of Maylor (1985).

that at large or small values of f_n, the system sensitivity to a small dot is lowest. Suppose that the cue instruction initiates a gradual, progressive reduction in f_n by switching out the largest filters. Sensitivity initially increases until only the optimum set of medium to small size filters are active, and then sensitivity falls again as f_n decreases further.

Now consider what happens while this is occurring, but in other parts of the visual field. The reason for controlling the larger filters is to regulate the data rate into the time-consuming spatial process. Suppose that it is actually the potential number of groups that is regulated. In the absence of specific knowledge concerning the image, the probable or expected number of groups is proportional to the size of the largest active filter. This means that switching out filters anywhere increases the potential number of groups, unless balanced by switching in elsewhere filters that are larger than those currently active. So as the largest filter size drops at the attended location, it must rise elsewhere, and consequently, these unattended locations will be less sensitive to the spot. They are indeed found to be slower (Posner et al. 1980).

Selection of Initial Spatial Scale (b)

Another experiment that supports the idea that the value of f_n is under high-level control comes from Duncan (1984). The basic stimulus of this study is shown in Fig. 5.9. It comprises an outline box with a gap on one side plus a tilted, dotted line running through the box. Subjects were shown this target very briefly and then asked to make judgements concerning: which side of the box (left or right) had the gap, whether the box was long or short; whether the line was dotted or dashed, and whether the line was tilted clockwise or anticlockwise from vertical.

Duncan compared subjects' accuracy when they were asked to make only one judgement with accuracy when asked to make two judgements. The basic finding was that the second judgement to be reported was worse, but only if it was about an attribute of a different stimulus element from the first judgement, i.e. when a box judgement was followed by a tilted line judgement, or vice versa. Joint responses about these two different elements of the stimulus appeared to conflict. In more detail, deterioration in performance was found for: (1) box size and box gap judgements when preceded by line tilt or line texture judgements; and (2) tilt judgements when preceded by box size or box gap judgements.

Figure 5.9 shows the zero-crossings and the MIRAGE zero-bounding contours for the Duncan stimulus. Figure 5.9 shows the zero-bounding contours for decreasing values of f_n, the largest filter space constant. Inspection of the individual filter zero-crossings is quite interesting. The largest filter only "sees" the box: There is no available information in its response concerning the line at all. This is because the line is unable to compete with the deep negative response of the filter that is being generated in the centre of the box by the two box sides. As the size of the filter decreases from the largest down to the smallest, more and more of the line becomes "visible". The texture of the line is only resolved in the smallest filter's output.

Inspection of the MIRAGE response zero-bounding contours is also interesting. The line orientation and texture are really only available when f_n is quite small. Box size and gap, on the other hand, are available at all values of f_n. However, they are available most rapidly for large f_n, because there are fewer elements in general to be processed the larger f_n is. Moreover, the data of Watt and Morgan (1984) show that spatial locations are measured more accurately by large filters than small ones. Box information is most useful at large f_n.

The system is compromised by conflicting requirements: Should it set itself up to operate at a fine spatial scale and receive accurate line information, or should it set itself with a larger value of f_n and receive good box information?

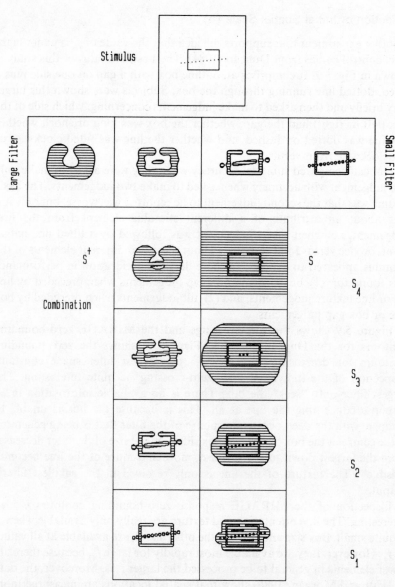

FIG. 5.9.   At the top is the stimulus used by Duncan (1984). Beneath this are the zero-crossings in the output of a range of different size second derivative Gaussian filters. At the bottom are shown the zero-bounding contours of the MIRAGE *S* signals.

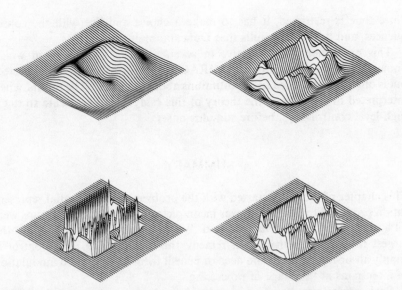

FIG. 5.9a. This shows the individual filter responses to the Duncan stimulus. The largest filter is on the top left, and the smaller filters are then placed clockwise round from there.

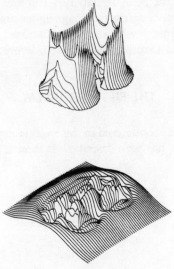

FIG. 5.9b. This shows the S signals from the Duncan stimulus of the previous figure. S^+ is on the top; S^- is on the bottom.

Since time is restricted, it has to make a choice and live with the consequences, and hence the results that Duncan obtained.

This experiment is instructive in several respects. The way in which "objectness" is produced by the MIRAGE transformation is not expected, but is obviously matched to our intuitions about "objects". The results, when interpreted in the light of the theory of this essay, clearly indicate strategic high-level control of f_n, before stimulus onset.

SUMMARY

This chapter of the essay started with the problem that the spatial representation produced by MIRAGE was incomplete: Elements within groups were all accorded the same group position. We have seen that switching out the largest filters progressively can remedy this shortcoming. The control is simply all-or-none; there is no need or benefit from sophisticated modulation of filter gains at this stage of processing.

Such control results in a hierarchical representation of spatial position, which in order to handle changes in the image efficiently requires a dynamic memory recording both the representation and its recent history of processing.

Control of f_n, the size of the largest filter into the summation step (3) of the MIRAGE transformation was used to account for the results of experiments by Treisman and Gelade (1980) and Eriksen and Eriksen (1974). This control is automatic, being initiated by stimulus onset or change, and proceeding asynchronously across the image under simple feedback. Control by intervention of higher levels was then discussed, and experiments by Posner et al. (1980) and Duncan (1984) were interpreted accordingly.

THE FIFTH PROBLEM

The final problem to be encountered in this essay is explanatory. The Primal Sketch, as I envisage it, has been described. Is there a good metaphor for its actions?

6

Synopsis: Low-level Vision as an Active Process

The central point for this essay was an algorithm, MIRAGE, derived from psychophysical measures of human sensitivity to edge blur, edge location, edge contrast, and similar parameters. The algorithm subserves three distinct types of functions. The first was essentially data compression: The infinite range of luminances is replaced by a smaller and more predictable range of contrasts, but in a manner that does not impose heavy signal-to-noise costs. The second was feature enhancement and finding: Edges, lines, corners, and intersections are all enhanced and may be simply found.

These first two functions are straightforward image-processing. Once the various features and image attributes have been found, they are measured, and it was necessary to consider the scales for measurement. In the cases of contour curvature and blur, it was asserted that the distributions of values found in natural scenes are not uniform. This allows the system to calibrate itself for these quantities and at the same provide a metric that is not arbitrary. This is not the case for contour position and for surface luminance; it is, however, the case for contour separations and for luminance contrasts. The visual system, it is argued, makes measurements of these derived quantities. The use of contour separation (distance and orientation) measurements is also a useful technique because these attributes can be used to define a two-dimensional pattern irrespective of its position in the visual field. The other affine transformations of rotation and dilation are also easy to measure and detect in such a representation. The final function concerned grouping and the processing strategy, whereby time-consuming spatial processes can be avoided if spatial position analysis is not necessary.

137

THE THREE NEW ARGUMENTS

This final function required three new arguments that followed on, one from another, from an inadequacy in the MIRAGE algorithm. A representation in terms of local spatial differences (distances, luminance contrasts, etc.) does not make explicit remote spatial differences, which therefore have to be inferred.

Calculating Spatial Positions

The *first new argument* concerned the nature and effect of errors in the local measurement of element separations and directions. The errors effectively prevent a precise solution for the spatial positions of the elements from being computed, and as a result a time-consuming constraint relaxation process is needed. It is relevant in this respect to note that discrimination judgements of line tilt and length are different in several respects from judgements of line shape. Accuracy in the shape case is determined by the basic spatial uncertainty in mapping from the retinal image, and information can be integrated at high efficiency along a considerable length of line segment (Watt, Ward, & Casco, 1987). In the case of line tilt and length, accuracy is not determined by this basic spatial uncertainty and is in general much lower (Watt, 1984). Thresholds for discriminating the orientation of a line or the implicit line defined by two dots are a fixed angular rotation irrespective of length, i.e. a fixed proportion of the length of the line or the separation of the elements. Likewise, thresholds for differences in line length or dot separation are a fixed proportion of the separation. These two proportions are of the same magnitude (about 1% and 3% respectively), and this means that, although the local measure of relative position is limited only by the fundamental mapping uncertainty, the global position has an uncertainty or fuzziness distributed around about the element. The size of this distribution is determined by how far away neighbouring elements are.

Automatic Time Sequence

The *second new argument* concerned the low-level control of grouping, with the suggestion that groups receive full spatial analysis, but the elements within a group are treated only statistically and topologically. There is some evidence for this; for example, the exact order of a series of parallel lines of differing luminance takes longer to judge than their number (Rentschler & Treutwein, 1985; see the comment in Watt, 1985). The "global effect" of saccadic eye movements is another instance (Coren & Hoenig, 1972; Findlay, 1982). When asked to move their eyes from a fixation marker to the nearer of a pair of lines in the periphery, subjects typically make a saccade first to a point midway between the two lines (i.e. the position of their group) and then move their eye back to the target. However, if the eye-movement response is delayed after the onset of the peripheral stimuli, there is a reduced tendency to do this, and if the saccade latency is over about 150 ms, subjects will saccade directly to the target (Findlay & Harris, in press). The delay allows time for the large filters to be switched out and position of the individual lines to be calculated.

The finding of Eriksen and Eriksen (1974) that the central letter of a group is identified or categorised more slowly when the outer ones (which are strictly irrelevant) are different than when they are the same as the central target, is also expected from the present argument. The three letters are initially a group and their individual identities are partially represented, but their spatial positions are not. If all three are the same, there is no need to discover which is the central target; if they differ, the grouping distance has to be reduced so that the identity of the centre letter can be analysed. Subjects experience the need to use selective attention.

High-level Control

The *third new argument* was that high-level control of the whole grouping and spatial representation process was simple to implement and would allow considerable choice of the nature of the final representation. Already in discussing the second new argument, the link between control of low-level vision and the conscious experience of selective attention has been made. The third argument forces us to regard the low-level vision process as a skilled activity rather than a strictly input-determined process. The argument is seductive because of its simplicity, but there is not much evidence that the control process hypothesised really exists.

One line of evidence came from the report of Posner et al. (1980) that the latency for the simple detection of the sudden appearance of a small spot of light could be reduced by providing an indication to the subject of where and roughly when it would appear. The cue to the subject initiates a process of progressively switching out the largest filters, changing the potential signal-to-noise ratio and producing concomitant response latency variations. The major finding was that a low-level visual task could be influenced by events that precede the stimulus and that may not even be visual, having only a semantic relationship to the target. A similar line of reasoning was indicated by the experiment of Duncan (1984).

It is worth noting that there is a superficial similarity between the present proposal and the idea of Julesz (Julesz, 1980; Julesz & Papathomas, 1984; Julesz & Schumer, 1981) that subjects can selectively attend to the different spatial frequencies (or scales) that are simultaneously present in a visual scene. However, the significant difference lies in the details of MIRAGE:

Selection is not explicitly per spatial frequency; the different spatial scales are treated differently at any given time; and there is an orderly sequence of moving through the spatial scales.

AN ANALOGY FOR THE PRIMAL SKETCH

It is often helpful to have a mental picture of a process, and I now offer a rather weak analogy for the Primal Sketch process. What are the salient architectural aspects of the Primal Sketch?

1. At the largest scale in operation at a particular moment it computes spatial positions.
2. At finer scales, if present, a statistical representation is applied.
3. Time permitting, the largest filters are switched out, adding finer detail to the representation of spatial position. Filter switches are all-or-none.
4. The starting and terminating values of the largest scale to be in operation can be set in advance by a high-level government.

Think of a railway signalman, sitting in a signalling box at a busy marshalling yard. Some trains, express passenger services, pass through very quickly and he must switch the points along the line to offer the train least resistance. As it passes he has little chance to do more than observe that a train passed, judge its overall length, and count the number of coaches. If the speed of the train imposes less time constraint, then he can switch the points to pass different portions of the train through different sidings, to weigh each coach or truck.

The actions of the signalman are governed by the speed of the train (the stimulus) and his task. The only actions that he can perform are all-or-none settings of points, which determine which portions of the train pass over which sections of the track (through which analytic processes). But he can control the timing of his actions, and thus determine the track usage.

RELATIONSHIPS BETWEEN LOW-LEVEL
VISION AND COGNITION

This discussion started with an algorithm and then proceeded to find increasingly high-level functions that are accomplished. It is possible to work in the opposite direction, and four cognitive functions of vision will now be considered.

Visual Attention

Many theories of visual attention are to be found (see Duncan, 1984, for a review). They all start with the proposition that at some stage in the visual process there is a capacity-limited step, through which parts of the image must proceed in a serial stream. Attention is seen as a selection process to segment the image into parts of a suitable size and then to determine the order in which the segments are processed. The main research interest concerns the level of processing at which the selection occurs and on what attributes the segmentation is based.

There are some new terms here: *capacity-limit, serial stream, level of processing*, which have not appeared before in this essay. They are rooted in a view of perception in which the sensory data proceed through a sequence of processes, each taking over the data when the previous process has been completed. Although such a simplistic view of perception would not be entertained now, many of the terms used to discuss visual attention indicate that it remains influential. The original view of perception was seen as necessary to account for the transition from the luminance image of a page of writing to a semantic understanding of the text. Attentional control of such a sequence of operations then seems natural: At some stage the information must pass from a signal-domain to a symbol-domain representation, and intuitively it seems reasonable to suppose that a serial item-by-item stage of processing might be called for. Within this framework there are two broadly distinct views: One that attention acts rather like a searchlight (Eriksen & Eriksen, 1974) and indiscriminately selects areas of retinal space early in the system for privileged processing; the other that attention is very discriminating and makes a late selection of that part of the image corresponding to an object (Neisser, 1967), perhaps even when two objects overlap in space (Duncan, 1984).

The difficulty with early selection is that areas of especial interest are most unlikely all to have the same size, shape, etc.: The searchlight would need some intelligence to match its beam to the particular image. This intelligence would have to be based on either information about what was in the image, which can only be obtained by processing the image, or information about what objects are in the scene, in which case it is really late selection. The difficulty with late selection is how the word "object" should be defined, perhaps the most acceptable definition being a unit to which selective attention is applied, which renders the argument circular. When we inspect a bare tree in winter, the structure (or object) that we see depends on the scale that our percept is based on: the overall shape, or the tangle of branches, or the markings on the bark. It depends on both the image and the state of the visual system.

The change of emphasis that this essay argues for concerns the relationship between low-level visual processing and higher-level cognitive functioning. It is claimed that low-level vision has a control structure and a representation that are both dynamic. The representation improves in a very specific fashion over time. If one interrupts the process of low-level vision in the course of building up its final and best representation, one will not find an orderly sequence of stages completed followed by another sequence of stages not completed. One will find a workable spatial representation at a particular spatial scale *plus* a non-spatial representation of finer spatial scales. Chapter 4 described a slow spatial process that can be by-passed if an impoverished representation will suffice, and Chapter 5 showed how control of this choice can be implemented. Chapter 4 described how the output of isotropic derivative filters preserves and enhances attributes that intuitively define "objectness". The outputs of such filters are inherently intelligent in so far as the filter design reflects this "objectness", and the spatial distribution of processing capacity can be decided on the basis of their outputs. It is crucial to this argument that the tasks of search, recognition (as in naming a word), and navigation can work on the types of partial representations that MIRAGE delivers.

Visual Search

Visual search for a specific object (the term is correctly used here) requires that the visual field be monitored for the appearance anywhere of some characteristic qualities of that object. The object of the search can be specified at different levels of generality: a car, a yellow car, a yellow Volkswagen car, etc. Usually the size of the object in three-space relative to its surroundings is determined, and this is important because it determines the scale at which the corresponding image will be formed.

The object can appear in the Primal Sketch representation in two forms, either as an isolated element or group, or as an element within a wider group. If it is an isolated group, then the degree of representation including its position will be fairly complete; if it is in a group, then the representation will be partial. The degree of success in searching will depend on how well matched the defining characteristics of the object are to the primitives of the Primal Sketch representation. The search will usually be faster and more efficient if the defining characteristics of the object are attributes that are determinants of grouping, such as colour.

Visual Recognition

Recognition involves the matching of two representations, one perceptual and one from memory. Many objects (the term is also correct at this level) are recognisable in principle with non-spatial representations. This is almost necessary to allow for the projective transformations of image formation and a degree of variation in the physical instantiation of objects: No two rose flowers are identical and no two views of the same rose flower are identical. Since some aspects of contour shape, geometric as well as topological, are available in the early partial representations, instances can nevertheless be distinguished rapidly. There is, however, the need to match the fidelity and completeness of the memory representation to that of the perceptual representation, and this rather implies that some aspects of memory have to be organised along similar lines to those discussed in this essay for perception.

Visual Navigation

Navigation is perhaps inherently an activity that requires spatial information, but often only at the larger spatial scales where bodies that we are likely to bump into may usually be found. Navigation is also a relatively slow process. All the bodies that are large enough to be important for actions planned and executed over a time scale of a few seconds will be within a few metres of the observer, and their retinal images will be large. Large images usually imply large spatial scales, and so speed of processing is optimum. It is interesting to consider what happens when these general constraints do not apply, as for example the navigation of a motor car down a busy high street. In this case, where actions are much faster than in walking, bodies that have small retinal images found in the finest spatial scales have high navigational importance, and the visual system is stretched, sometimes to the limit of its processing speed. Many drivers have experienced the difficulty of "reading the road ahead" when faced with dense and irregular traffic flow, high numbers of traffic signs, bright advertisement hoardings and shop windows, reflections on a wet road surface, and so on. Although none of these factors impairs vision totally, put together, they make a scene where, for speed considerations, the visual system will be forced to make heavy use of non-spatial representations that are of little use for this particular task. There is an applied value to the subject matter of this essay to be explored and exploited.

CODA: THE LOGIC OF THIS ESSAY

In this essay, I have described a model for vision that begins with the reflection of light at surfaces and ends with control of the nature of the spatial representations that are created. There has been a single logic throughout that has related visual processes to what was required of a Primal Sketch processor.

In order to define the requirements of the Primal Sketch, it was necessary to note that in our physical environment, matter tends to be clumped into quasi-rigid bodies. The surfaces of such bodies reflect and scatter light. Bodies do not have fuzzy surfaces, and as a result, their occluding contours tend to be projected as luminance discontinuities into the retinal image. The shape of the surface of such bodies may be smoothly curved or creased. The reflectance of the surface of any one body may vary so that the surface is marked with texture. The spatial scale of texture is finer than that of the surfaces it covers. With this set of constraints, it is possible to require that the Primal Sketch detect and characterise as many occluding edges and creases as possible. The texture markings on surfaces should also be represented by the Primal Sketch.

The model that has been described in these pages can be traced back in every instance to this set of constraints and requirements. So, for example, the sensitivity of the Primal Sketch to line intersections, which is obviously of crucial importance in letter identification and reading, can be traced back to the requirement that our visual system detect occlusions in the scene.

Let me offer a few words on the status of the arguments of this essay. The MIRAGE model is a valid model for the psychophysics that is available. It is also based on sound computational theory. Therefore, I regard Chapters 1 to 4 as being an approximate model of reality, in the scientific tradition. Chapter 5, which related the MIRAGE scheme to the various paradigms and phenomena known collectively as visual attention, is more speculative. I argue that the Primal Sketch theory and MIRAGE algorithm offer a sufficient explanation for the phenomena, but would not claim them as a necessary explanation. The theory that has been described will not stand or fall according to its ability to explain these types of phenomena. The term "visual attention" may cover a multitude of different control processes in addition to those described here. Many of the experiments conducted in this area are very blunt tools for my purposes. This is because they were designed within a particular framework of how visual perception might be, which is different from the one I have explored. My impression is that it will be surprising and possibly challenging for cognitive psychologists to discover that early visual processes deliver a distinctively structured representation and require control.

The approach that I have adopted and described in this essay leads to a characteristic way of *understanding* what it is to see. It is an approach that owes a great deal to the philosophy behind the work of David Marr. It aims to understand the visual system as a device that has been designed to perform particular tasks in a particular environment. A task is built from three components: the present state, some desired future state, the mechanism for effecting the desired change in state. We shall eventually need full physical descriptions of what those tasks are, what the environment is, and the design.

The full philosophy of this approach and how all the various aspects of vision relate to it are the subject of a book I am presently preparing entitled *Understanding vision.*

There is another type of understanding, which can be regarded as metapsychological. When our mind determines and invokes a particular course of control over low-level vision, what we experience may be the intention followed by the act of attending to a particular object or location in space. This experience is the mind's own model of its actions. This mental model is perhaps best described with physical metaphors such as searchlights or perhaps with semantic concepts such as attention, objects, or features. It is important to realise that these are not part of a physical understanding of visual processing; they are part of an understanding of our own personal internal mental understanding of our actions in seeing things. Of course, such metapsychological factors would become a necessary part of a physical understanding of vision if, but only if, they actually *determined* what control processes were available at any one time rather than merely *representing* what control processes were available. This may well be the case in young children who have yet to learn how to see with the highest possible efficiency. It may well also be true for most of us of the periphery of the visual field, with which we are less practised and less skilled at seeing than we are with the central one degree of the visual field.

References

Andrews, D.P. (1964) Error-correcting perceptual mechanisms. *Quarterly Journal of Experimental Psychology, 16*, 104–115.

Bashinski, H.S. & Bacharach, V.R. (1980) Enhancement of perceptual sensitivity as the result of selectively attending to spatial locations. *Perception & Psychophysics*, 28, 241–280.

Blakemore, C.B. & Campbell, F.W. (1969) On the existence of neurones in the human visual system selectively sensitive to the orientation and size of retinal images. *Journal of Physiology (London), 203*, 237–260.

Blakemore, C.B. & Sutton, P. (1969) Size adaptations: A new after effect. *Science, 166*, 245–247.

Burton, G.J. & Moorhead, I.R. (in press) Colour and spatial structure in natural scenes. *Applied Optics*.

Campbell, F.W. & Robson, J. (1968) Application of Fourier analysis to the visibility of gratings. *Journal of Physiology (London), 197*, 551–566.

Canny, J. (1984) *Finding edges and lines in images*. M.I.T. AI. Lab. Tech. Report. 720.

Carter, B.E. & Henning, G.B. (1971) The detection of gratings in narrow-band visual noise. *Journal of Physiology (London), 219*, 355–365.

Coren, S. & Hoenig, P. (1972) Effect of non-target stimuli upon the length of voluntary saccades. *Perceptual and Motor Skills, 34*, 499–508.

Cornsweet, T. (1970) *Visual Perception*. New York: Academic Press.

Duncan, J. (1984) Selective attention and the organization of visual information. *Journal of Experimental Psychology (General), 113*, 501–517.

Eriksen, B.A. & Eriksen, C.W. (1974) Effects of noise letters upon the identification of a target letter in a non-search task. *Perception & Psychophysics, 16*, 143–149.

Findlay, J. (1982) Global processing for saccadic eye movements. *Vision Research, 21*, 347–354.

Findlay, J.M. & Harris, L.R. (in preparation) Saccadic eye movements to single and double targets.

Foley, J.M. & Legge, G.E. (1981) Contrast detection and near-threshold discrimination in human vision. *Vision Research, 21*, 1041–1053.

Gibson, J.J. (1933) Adaptation, after effect and contrast in the perception of curved lines. *Journal of Experimental Psychology, 16*, 1–31.

Graham, N. & Nachmias, J. (1971) Detection of grating patterns containing two spatial frequencies: A comparison of single-channel and multiple-channels models. *Vision Research, 11*, 251–259.

Graham, N., Robson, J.G., & Nachmias, J. (1978) Grating summation in fovea and periphery. *Vision Research, 18*, 815–825.

Gregory, R.L. & Heard, P.F. (1979) Border locking and the café wall illusion. *Perception, 8*, 365–380.

Gregory, R.L. & Heard, P.F. (1983) Visual dissociations of movement, position, and stereo depth: Some phenomenal phenomena. *Quarterly Journal of Experimental Psychology, 35A*, 217–237.

Henning, G.B., Hertz, B.G., & Broadbent, D.E. (1975) Some experiments bearing on the hypothesis that the visual system analyzes patterns in independent bands of spatial frequency. *Vision Research, 15*, 887–899.

Jamar, J.H.T. & Koenderink, J.J. (1985) Contrast detection and detection of contrast modulation for noise gratings. *Vision Research, 25*, 511–521.

Julesz, B. (1980) Spatial frequency channels in one-, two- and three-dimensional vision: Variations on an auditory theme by Bekesy. In C.S. Harris (Ed.), *Visual coding and adaptability*. Hillsdale, N.J.: Lawrence Erlbaum Associates Inc.

Julesz, B. (1981) Textons, the elements of texture perception and their interactions. *Nature, 290*, 91–97.

Julesz, B. & Papathomas, T.V. (1984) On spatial-frequency channels and attention. *Perception & Psychophysics, 36*, 398–399.

Julesz, B. & Schumer, R.A. (1981) Early visual perception. *Annual Review of Psychology, 32*, 575–627.

Kahn, J.I. and Foster, D.H. (1981) Visual comparison of rotated and reflected random-dot patterns as a function of their positional symmetry and separation in the field. *Quarterly Journal of Experimental Psychology, 33A*, 155–166.

Koenderink, J. (1984). The structure of images. *Biological Cybernetics, 50*, 363–370.

Laming, D.R.J. (1986) *Sensory analysis*. London: Academic Press.

Legge, G.E. & Foley, J.M. (1980) Contrast masking in human vision. *Journal of the Optical Society of America, 70*, 1458–1471.

Legge, G.E. & Kersten, D. (1983) Light and dark bars: contrast discrimination. *Vision Research, 23*, 473–483.

MacKerras, P., Bossomaier, T., & Laughlin, S. (in preparation) Information gains from contrast adaptation.

Marr, D.C. (1976) Early processing of visual information. *Philosophical Transactions of the Royal Society (B), 275*, 483–524.

Marr, D.C. (1977) Analysis of occluding contour. *Proceedings of the Royal Society of London (B), 197*, 441–475.

Marr, D.C. (1982) *Vision*. San Francisco: W.H. Freeman and Co.

Marr, D.C. & Hildreth, E. (1980) A theory of edge detection. *Proceedings of the Royal Society of London (B), 207*, 187–217.

Marr, D.C. & Nishihara, H.K. (1978) Representation and recognition of the spatial organization of three-dimensional shapes. *Proceedings of the Royal Society of London (B), 200*, 269–294.

Marr, D.C. & Poggio, T. (1979) A computational theory of human stereo vision. *Proceedings of the Royal Society of London (B), 204*, 301–328.

Marr, D.C. & Ullman, S. (1981) Directional selectivity and its use in early visual processing. *Proceedings of the Royal Society of London (B)*, *211*, 151–180.

Mather, G. & Morgan, M.J. (1986) Irradiation: Implications for theories of edge localisation. *Vision Research*, *26*, 1007–1016.

Maylor, E.A. (1985) Facilitatory and inhibitory components of orienting in visual space. In M.I. Posner & O.S.M. Mann (Eds.), *Attention and performance XI*, 189–204. Hillsdale, N.J.: Lawrence Erlbaum Associates Inc.

Morgan, M.J. & Watt, R.J. (1982). Mechanisms of interpolation in human spatial vision. *Nature*, *299*, 553–555.

Morgan, M.J. & Watt, R.J. (1984) Spatial frequency interference effects and interpolation in vernier acuity. *Vision Research*, *24*, 1911–1919.

Moulden, B. & Renshaw, J. (1979) The Munsterberg illusion and "irradiation". *Perception*, *8*, 275–301.

Nachmias, J. & Rogovitz, B.E. (1983) Masking by spatially modulated gratings. *Vision Research*, *23*, 1621–1629.

Nachmias, J. & Sansbury, R. (1974) Grating contrast: discrimination may be better than detection. *Vision Research*, *14*, 1039–1042.

Neisser, U. (1967) *Cognitive psychology*. New York: Appleton-Century, Crofts.

Pearson, D.E. & Robinson, J.A. (1985) Visual communication at very low data rates. *Proceedings of the Institute of Electronic and Electrical Engineers*, *73*, 795–812.

Pelli, D.G. (1985) Uncertainty explains many aspects of visual contrast detection and discrimination. *Journal of the Optical Society of America*, *2A*, 15-8–1531.

Posner, M.I., Snyder, C.R.R., & Davidson, B.J. (1980) Attention and the detection of signals. *Journal of Experimental Psychology (General)*, *109*, 106–174.

Rentschler, I. & Treutwein, B. (1985) Loss of spatial phase relationships in extrafoveal vision. *Nature*, *313*, 308–310.

Sachs, M.B., Nachmias, J., & Robson, J.G. (1971) Spatial frequency channels in human vision. *Journal of the Optical Society of America*, *61*, 1176–1186.

Spacek, L. (1985) The detection of contours and their visual motion. Unpublished Ph.D. thesis, Univ. of Essex.

Srinivasan, M.V., Laughlin, S.B., & Dubs, A. (1982) Predictive coding: A fresh view of inhibition in the retina. *Proceedings of the Royal Society of London (B)*, *216*, 427–459.

Stevens, K.A. (1981) The visual interpretation of surface contours. *Artificial Intelligence*, *17*, 47–73.

Stromeyer, C.F. III & Julesz, B. (1972) Spatial frequency masking in vision: Critical bands and spread of masking. *Journal of the Optical Society of America*, *62*, 1221–1232.

Treisman, A.M. & Gelade, G. (1980) A feature-integration theory of attention. *Cognitive Psychology*, *12*, 97–136.

Watt, R.J. (1984) Towards a general theory of the visual acuities for shape and spatial arrangement. *Vision Research*, *24*, 1377–1386.

Watt, R.J. (1985) Structured representation in low-level vision. *Nature*, *313*, 266–267.

Watt, R.J. (1987) Scanning from coarse to fine spatial scales in the human vision system after the onset of a stimulus. *Journal of the Optical Society of America*, *4A*, 2006–2021.

Watt, R.J. & Morgan, M.J. (1983) The recognition and representation of edge blur: Evidence for spatial primitives in human vision. *Vision Research*, *23*, 1457–1477.

Watt, R.J. & Morgan, M.J. (1984) Spatial filters and the localization of luminance changes in human vision. *Vision Research*, *24*, 1387–1397.

Watt, R.J. & Morgan, M.J. (1985) A theory of the primitive spatial code in human vision. *Vision Research*, *25*, 1661–1674.

Watt, R.J., Ward, R.M., & Casco, C. (1987) The detection of deviation from straightness in lines. *Vision Research*, *27*, 1659–1678.

Wilson, H.R. (1983) Psychophysical evidence for spatial channels. In O.J. Braddick & A.C. Sleigh (Eds.), *Physical and biological processing of images*. Berlin: Springer-Verlag.

Author Index

Subject Index

Some Recent and Forthcoming Titles in
Essays in Cognitive Psychology

Philip Barnard: *Human-Computer Interaction*
*Vicki Bruce: *Recognising Faces* (February 1988)
Dick Byrne: *Cognitive Maps of the Environment*
Anne Cutler: *Comparative Psycholinguistics*
Michael Eysenck and Andrew Matthews: *Anxiety: The Cognitive Perspective*
Giovanni Flores D'Arcais: *Language Comprehension*
James Hampton: *Concepts*
Leslie Henderson: *The Flow Diagram in Cognitive Psychology*
Graham Hitch and Sebastian Halliday: *Children's Working Memory*
Charles Hulme and Susan Mackenzie: *Working Memory in Mental Sub-normality*
Mark Keane: *Analogical Thinking*
William Marslen-Wilson: *Spoken Word Recognition*
Roy Patterson: *Spiral Patterns of Sound*
Patrick Rabbitt: *IQ Test Scores and Cognitive Models*
Marcus Taft: *The Mental Lexicon*
John Teasdale: *Cognitive Psychotherapy*
William Wagenaar: *Paradoxes of Gambling Behaviour*
*Roger Watt: *Visual Processing: Computational, Physiological and Cognitive Research* (February 1988)

*Asterisked titles were published, or were about to be published, at the time this list was produced. For further information about these, or any of the other titles, please contact the publisher, Lawrence Erlbaum Associates Ltd., 27 Palmeira Mansions, Church Road, Hove, East Sussex BN3 2FA, U.K. (Tel: 0273 207411). American and Canadian orders should be addressed to the New Jersey office: Lawrence Erlbaum Associates Inc., 365 Broadway, Hillsdale, New Jersey, 07642 U.S.A. (Tel: 201 666 4110).